YOUTUBE SECRET 2023

HOW TO GROW YOUR YOUTUBE CHANNEL AND START MAKING MONEY AS A VIDEO INFLUENCER

By

JIMMY BAKER

© **Copyright 2022. All Rights Reserved.**

The publication is sold with the idea that the publisher is not required to render accounting, officially permitted or otherwise qualified services. This document is geared towards providing exact and reliable information concerning the topic and issue covered. If advice is necessary, legal or professional, a practiced individual in the profession should be ordered.
- From a Declaration of Principles which was accepted and approved equally by a Committee of the American Bar Association and a Committee of Publishers and Associations.

In no way is it legal to reproduce, duplicate, or transmit any part of this document in either electronic means or printed format. Recording of this publication is strictly prohibited, and any storage of this document is not allowed unless with written permission from the publisher—all rights reserved.

The information provided herein is stated to be truthful and consistent. Any liability, in terms of inattention or otherwise, by any usage or abuse of any policies, processes, or directions contained within is the sole and utter responsibility of the recipient reader. Under no circumstances will any legal responsibility or blame be held against the publisher for any reparation, damages, or monetary loss due to the information herein, either directly or indirectly.

Respective authors own all copyrights not held by the publisher.

The information herein is offered for informational purposes solely and is universal as so. The presentation of the information is without a contract or any guarantee assurance.

The trademarks that are used are without any consent, and the publication of the trademark is without permission or backing by the trademark owner. All trademarks and brands within this book are for clarifying purposes only and are owned by the owners themselves, not affiliated with this document

TABLE OF CONTENTS

PART ONE: BLUEPRINT 7

    INTRODUCTION 8

    BE FEARLESS AND IGNITE YOUR PASSION 10

    HOW DOES YOUTUBE WORK? 13

    YOUTUBE CHANNEL MEMBERSHIPS 19

    YOUTUBE SECURITY TIPS 26

    QUALITIES OF A SUCCESSFUL YOUTUBE CHANNEL 28

    HOW TO SET UP YOUR YOUTUBE CHANNEL . 34

    CREATING GOOD CONTENT FOR YOUR CHANNEL 37

    INTERACTING WITH YOUR VIEWERS AND YOUTUBERS ALIKE 40

    HOW TO SHOOT AND PICK YOUR IDEAL CAMERA 45

THE BEST TOOLS TO GROW AND MAKE MONEY FROM YOUR YOUTUBE CHANNEL 54

HOW TO UPLOAD A VIDEO TO YOUTUBE, STEP BY STEP 80

THE IDEAL SIZE AND DIMENSIONS FOR YOUTUBE VIDEOS 86

HOW TO MAKE YOUTUBE SHORTS 92

HOW TO LIVE STREAM ON YOUTUBE 105

YOUTUBE MONEY-MAKING TIPS 129

HOW TO MONETIZE YOUR CONTENT 133

PART TWO: STRATEGY 143

THE PERFECT VIDEO RECIPE 144

ATTRACTING YOUR IDEAL AUDIENCE ON AUTOPILOT 161

GROWING YOUR AUDIENCE WITH COLLABORATION 169

FOLLOW YOUTUBE TRENDS TO KEEP UP 176

YOUTUBE GUIDELINES FOR MONETIZING CONTENT 178

HOW TO INCREASE VIEWERS AND EARN MORE MONEY 183

YOUTUBE SELLING ADVICE 189

HOW VIDEOS CAN HELP YOUR BUSINESS GROW 194

HOW TO MARKET YOUR CHANNEL 199

SCALE YOUR VISION AND THINK DIFFERENTLY 206

YOUTUBE MARKETING SECRETS. 211

YOUR KEY MARKETING MESSAGE IS YOUTUBE ANALYTICS. 218

YOUTUBE SECRETS: HOW TO USE YOUTUBE MARKETING TO START A TIDAL WAVE OF SALES 226

NEW YOUTUBE FEATURES 231

CONCLUSION 240

PART ONE: BLUEPRINT

INTRODUCTION

One of the internet's most inventive uses is now YouTube. It is incredibly simple to use and boasts the widest range of subscribers who watch everything from the absurd to the everyday.

One of the best ways to communicate is through video, whether for internal communications, a product demo, or a web video for your YouTube channel.

As the second most frequently used search engine, YouTube is a natural destination for those in need of professional advice or instructional materials.

Establishing your expertise and building a loyal following for your paid services and products can be accomplished by posting helpful videos to YouTube at no cost to your audience. As a result, YouTube can be a lucrative business platform.

Internet video is a rapidly expanding phenomenon. Video streaming accounts for an astounding 37% of all Internet usage. Even subpar videos are prominently shown in search results on YouTube, which has more than 1 billion members and receives an average of 4 billion views daily. Without even considering the myriad of additional video-sharing websites like Vimeo, Flickr, and Bloomfire. The potential for video on the internet keeps expanding, with even Instagram and Pinterest lately joining the party.

Self-made celebrities of the internet age often gain followers by posting videos to social media that aim to inform, entertain, or review a product or service.

Even if you didn't start a YouTube channel to make money, you might change your mind once you see how many opportunities there are. Luckily, YouTube can be profited from in several creative ways.

Your audience has the power to make or break your YouTube channel, just like it does for Instagram influencers and bloggers. While true, starting a second business or side gig can increase your financial success.

BE FEARLESS AND IGNITE YOUR PASSION

Have you ever worked a job that you didn't enjoy? Even if it paid well, you might not have been all that interested in it. Similar rules apply when beginning a YouTube channel. Finding a specialty, subject, interest, or pastime you're passionate about is essential; otherwise, you'll lose enthusiasm, inspiration, and motivation, and it will die out after a few weeks.

Passion is a strong and scarcely manageable feeling. It is a strong, overpowering, or passionate sentiment or conviction. When you are enthusiastic about anything, it shows in your interactions with friends and family. You have more energy and enthusiasm. Getting closer to your potential and opening the doors to achievement will help you overcome your worries.

You don't need to hunt for passion since you already have it inside of you. List all activities you now like doing or have in the past. You become so enthused that you can't stop talking or thinking about it.

For instance, I enjoy skiing, martial arts, hiking, running, swimming, writing, creating videos, spending time with family and friends, exploring nature, traveling, and using technology.

To create a YouTube channel centered around your hobby, you should consider whether other people share your passion. Type in your primary keyword to find the top channels in your niche on YouTube. Visit online discussion boards, Facebook groups, and periodicals, and use Google and YouTube's autosuggest features to find relevant words to your core term. Then, you can use these key phrases to produce a series of videos for your Channel.

You'll experience many setbacks and difficulties as you follow your passion. This is natural; accept the difficulties because they will broaden your knowledge and enable you to assist someone facing a similar challenge along the route. They will be appreciative.

Thomas Edison failed a thousand times before he hit upon the solution that finally made his light bulb a success. His educators deemed him "too stupid to learn anything." Both of his previous employment opportunities ended due to his "non-productivity." Err often.

Your passion will succeed if you put all your effort and focus into it. Success can be measured in modest increments, such as the first 100 subscriptions or the first 100 views.

Your achievements will increase as you put more time and effort into them.

A YouTube channel with consistent video uploads is a fantastic way to get your name out there and attract new visitors to your website.

Giving something your entire concentration and power will ignite something within you. Until you attempt something new, you may never know what will ignite the tiny flame of passion that already burns within you.

HOW DOES YOUTUBE WORK?

There is no doubting the value of video in online business marketing. I've seen many people use YouTube to engage with prospects by providing extra content, but frequently they're doing it completely wrong. They have no idea what they're missing when using YouTube. Read on for my eight pieces of advice on how to use YouTube for video uploads.

VIDEO.

You want to post videos with a lot of valuable content. It's similar to writing an essay where you want to offer your finest advice or knowledge about an idea. The length is challenging. Although 15-minute videos have just been made possible on YouTube, I would rarely suggest making one unless it is perhaps footage from an event where it can truly convey the tale AND provide substance and value to the audience. I advise keeping it to no more than five minutes, ideally three to four.

Additionally, make sure the video is of high quality. In other words, the video, sound, and lighting are all of the highest calibers. How to ensure all of this is in place will be covered in more detail later. For the time being, though, just take my word that a high-quality YouTube video is one of the most important parts of your video.

CHANNEL.

Before you start uploading lots of videos, make sure to create your channel name. Consider this to be your domain or YouTube URL for your videos. In my opinion, an individual's channel name is preferable to a brand or corporation name. When you consider that the videos you upload are probably of you and not necessarily of other businesses or items, a personal channel name is more appealing. You may also alter your channel's design to make it simpler for viewers to browse and choose the videos you've uploaded for them to watch.

BRANDING.

I think branding your YouTube channel is really important. It elevates your channel by giving it a more polished appearance. The channel name is sufficient, but if you have the chance to add your logo and a few of your colors—possibly from your website or blog—why not do so? Several services are available to help you professionally brand your Twitter profile and Facebook fan page in addition to your YouTube channel. I prefer Twitter Backgrounds, personally.

Branding is crucial as the means through which the public connects virtually to your YouTube channel. Additionally, branding increases the authority of your Channel, helps users recognize it, and increases viewership. Your YouTube channel has four locations where branding is required.

- The small graphic or emblem that serves as your Channel's symbol.
- A sizable header banner on the site of the YouTube channel,
- A brief description under the "About" tab
- A channel trailer is shown to those who are not subscribed.

NAME.

One of the major errors individuals commit when uploading videos is this. Your camera or computer will give the video file a generic name when you finish recording it and upload it from your computer, such as MOV 0098765.mov or ABC 12345a.MOV. This name will appear on YouTube when you post it, which is not what you want! Always use a title for your video that is specific, descriptive, and pertinent to the content of the video. If you've previously submitted a video, you can quickly go back and change it by giving it a more informative and pertinent name.

DESCRIPTION.

You should apply a pertinent and instructive video name before adding the description. The description is more room for you to elaborate on the video's subject, benefits, and appeal than the name. Be descriptive, but avoid turning it into a book. You want it to be brief, clear, and straight to the point. Remember to put your website's URL at the start of every video you post so that viewers can see it first when watching video search results. YouTube will make the URL in the description you added clickable, enabling users to access your website or blog right away by clicking the link (and perhaps watch other videos or join your list.)

TAGS.

Using tags is one of the finest tricks for making your YouTube videos easily searchable. Similar to keywords are tags. They set the scene for what your video is about, making it simple for individuals looking for similar videos to find yours. Similar to how people search for websites on Google using keywords, users use tags on YouTube to find videos. Your tags should be as precise and well-defined as your keywords. It will be challenging to compete with terms like success or marketing. The most popular videos with those tags will be shown first. However, using more precise tags with space around them will be helpful. For instance, when I tag my videos with "authentic internet marketing," they frequently appear at the top of video search results. Instead of just Jimmy Baker, the " " quote should always be used with your name so that it searches for " Jimmy Baker."

SHARING.

YouTube has several wonderful capabilities for sharing your video with other social networks like Facebook and Twitter. You can decide whether to connect those social networks to your account when you upload your video so that any videos you upload will immediately be broadcast and published to those accounts, informing your followers that the video is ready for viewing. Additionally, you can "Like" and "Share" the video on social media sites for others to see.

EMBED.

Using the embed tool, you can upload your video to your website or blog. Use your video as soon as it has been posted! People will click on the video to return to YouTube, watch more of your videos, and view more of the content and information you have to provide because it makes it possible for them to view the content elsewhere outside of YouTube.

When using YouTube and adding your videos, take advantage of these tips and tricks, as they will help you expand your list, interact with people in a way that no other medium can, and eventually bring in new customers.

YOUTUBE CHANNEL MEMBERSHIPS

YouTubers always want to monetize their content.

You may consider adding YouTube channel memberships to earn extra money from your content without much extra work.

YouTube Channel Memberships were launched in 2018 to help creators reward their most devoted fans. Monthly members get behind-the-scenes footage, Q&As, and merchandise discounts.

They can also contribute to YouTubers' success.

Creators get a new revenue stream, and fans get access to their favorite content.

CHANNEL MEMBERSHIP PERKS

Channel Memberships let you offer subscribers exclusive perks. This can include:

- Custom Emojis
- Loyalty badges
- Community-only posts

- Live streams
- Real-time chat
- Extras.

The key is to offer exclusive content to your loyal members to make them feel special.

YOUTUBE MEMBERSHIP REQUIREMENTS

Adding memberships to your channel makes you a YouTube partner. To turn it on for your channel, you must meet additional requirements.

YouTube Channel Memberships are open to these creators:

- Join Youtube Partner
- 1000+ subscribers.
- Operate in a YouTube-approved country, such as the U.S., U.K., Japan, etc.
- Create non-kid-friendly content.
- Your channel must have some demonetized videos.
- Accept YouTube's rules.

YOUTUBE PREMIUM VS. CHANNEL MEMBERS.

Channel members and YouTube Premium subscribers often confuse creators and viewers.

- YouTube Premium offers an ad-free experience, offline video downloads, and free YouTube Music.
- A Premium subscription affects your Android, iPhone, iOS, and all other YouTube app experiences.
- Creators get paid based on how many Premium members watch their content since there are no ads.
- Channel membership benefits your favorite YouTube creators. For creators, fans pay for memberships directly.

HOW DO YOUTUBE SUBSCRIPTIONS WORK?

Youtube Channel Memberships offer "tiers" to join. Higher tiers cost more and offer better perks.

It's like Twitch, where subscribers get exclusive content.

YouTube used to set the prices for each membership level, but as of December 2021, you can set your own. YouTube suggests low, middle, and high prices.

Suppose you can attract more members at $2.99 per month; set your lowest price there. Each level requires 1-5 perks.

WHAT IS MEMBERSHIP GIFTING?

Gifting memberships sounds like it. Your subscribers can buy "bulk" memberships and give them away. Someone who watches the channel regularly can buy 15 memberships and distribute 14 of them to other people who enjoy the content.

It's an easy way to get more paid members. You need wealthy super-fans to give you channel memberships.

YOUTUBE MEMBERSHIP COSTS

Free memberships have a cost: YouTube takes 30% of profits.

Consider a $4.99 membership tier. At 100 members, you'll make $500. $350 is your profit.

$150 for YouTube.

It's a lot. And it rises with income. After 1000 subscribers, you'll send Youtube $1500 a month.

That extra money could be better spent reinvesting in your business or rewarding yourself.

Independent video memberships allow you to keep more of your earnings than YouTube Channel Memberships.

This is the way to go if you're an artist and want to sell memberships but don't have 30,000 subscribers.

If you're a creator on YouTube and want to make some money, you should get a Channel Membership.

YouTube Channel Memberships can be used alongside sponsored content and advertising without much work. Create custom emojis and upload bonus content.

Customers like you as a creator, so this works.

They're behind you.

They consider their monthly payment a donation.

YouTube Channel Memberships have drawbacks, like most things.

- **YouTube-friendly:** You'll lose 30% of your income.
- **YouTube's prices frequently change.** YouTube Channel Memberships face demonetization.
- You'll need YouTube's algorithm to attract new subscribers. Losing control of your income growth can result.

- You'll spend time and effort converting viewers into paying members, but you may lose them.

It's better to have membership platforms with benefits like YouTube but more control.

YOUTUBE SECURITY TIPS

YouTube is great if you like producing videos and videos. However, there are several safety measures you ought to think about. Posting the videos is acceptable as long as it's done correctly and safely.

You should first safeguard your identity. Keep your real name a secret. Don't divulge your home address, which can be used to trace you. Don't mention the name of your town or city either. Numerous spammers and hackers might quickly locate you. You may get into problems if they object to something in your video.

Since its launch, YouTube has become more and more well-known. Now, viewers may rate your videos. In addition, they can comment. They can discuss your videos with others. Keep your information private even if you become close to someone you met on YouTube. Try not to make any contacts if you receive any private messages. Maintain a nice demeanor if you are a featured person in the video. Never believe anyone you find online.

Make sure to respect others' privacy when recording them on camera. Don't provide any information about your friends and family members featured in the videos. Do not also break any copyrights. Music and motion pictures both have copyrights. These include sharing TV show snippets. You can get into legal problems for this. Lastly, don't let your enjoyment prevent you from uploading videos to YouTube. You will be fine as long as you are cautious. Indeed, many people may develop an addiction to YouTube.

QUALITIES OF A SUCCESSFUL YOUTUBE CHANNEL

Since its founding in February 2005, YouTube—the second-most viewed website in the world behind Google—has advanced significantly. Over one billion individuals use YouTube, or one-third of all internet users, and that one billion hours of videos are watched daily indicates how influential YouTube is in people's lives. The fact that YouTube is "a one-stop solution for everything people are looking for" makes it so popular.

Video lovers, sometimes known as YouTubers, are drawn to and given many possibilities by YouTube to display their skills and originality. Broad categories, including cooking, arts and crafts, gaming, beauty, education, entertainment, travel, etc., are used to group the videos published on YouTube. Successful YouTubers have wisely utilized this platform, which has brought them success (millions of followers) and income (millions of dollars) that they may not have ever dreamed of.

Any corporate video content developed, published, and shared online must be professional, content-rich, and accurately reflect your brand identity. Anything less could potentially harm your brand and not be an exercise that would improve it. Establishing confidence and trust in your brand's offering requires a cinematic, glossy, professional finish that looks appealing and contains all the necessary information. To reflect the professional aspect of your company, make sure your video was expertly created.

One of the key qualities of great YouTubers is the ability to stand out from the competition. They offer a unique product that hasn't been offered through other outlets.

It is understandable why so many individuals think about launching their own YouTube channel, given that there are more than a billion viewers and hundreds of millions of hours of daily viewing. The platform allows you to access a sizable worldwide audience as an individual or a company, enabling you to develop your brand and profit from ad income. However, submitting videos and hoping for the best won't work because of the intense competition. A well-thought-out plan is necessary to build your channel truly. The following advice can help you get off to a good start and slowly and continuously increase your subscriber base.

CREATE A CONCEPT

An unfocused channel will find it difficult to grow an audience. Therefore you should think about your goals immediately. Today, YouTube is a fully developed platform with many useful examples. Whether it's comedy routines, video game reviews, or makeup instructions, the most well-known video creators almost always have a specific goal. Although you don't have to stick to just one kind of video, viewers should be able to understand what you have to offer right away.

MAINTAIN EACH VIDEO'S FOCUS

Additionally, the videos should be targeted; rambling videos are more likely to lose viewers. While keeping videos brief is a good idea, longer ones can be successful if they are worth the extra time. Consider whether you have eliminated everything unneeded throughout the edit rather than concentrating too much on the duration. Prioritize the important topics, keep your edits crisp, and plan out your films.

KEYWORDS AND TRENDS FOR RESEARCH

Finding effective keywords can help you reach a wider audience, just like effective SEO. You should strive to add a keyword to assist your rank while making your title and description understandable. With more videos showing up near the top of the screen, targeting specific keywords can also help you rank in the search engines. Finding terms with a lot of searches is made easier with the Google keyword tool. To produce videos that satisfy a need, Google Trends can also assist you in identifying niche trends.

REQUEST LIKES AND SUBSCRIPTIONS FROM VIEWERS

It's possible that you have noticed calls for subscribers and likes if you watch a lot of videos. It may feel awkward to ask directly for something of this nature, but it works. Your likes and subscriber numbers should increase with just a simple reminder; there's no need to be pushy. The ideal course of action is still to request the support of your viewers rather than relying on individuals to remember or act of their own volition. Use annotations to add text to the screen that enhances the experience while subtly encouraging viewers to subscribe and enjoy the video.

INCLUDE OTHER SOCIAL MEDIA PLATFORMS IN YOUR INTEGRATION

Establishing your reputation on various platforms should be a part of developing your channel. Many people enjoy watching videos but might not consider becoming channel subscribers. Building a recognizable name through social media platforms increases the likelihood of people remembering you. Create an easy way for people to follow you across multiple platforms by linking all your social media profiles.

BE PERSISTENT AND PATIENT.

Millions of views are possible with a viral hit, but they are hard to forecast. Audiences may become irritated by attempts to create a viral hit since they are more aware of marketing ploys. Instead, concentrate on creating consistently high-quality content to grow your audience over time. Make an effort to plan a manageable schedule that will satisfy your audience. Establishing a successful channel can take time, but the viewers will appreciate hearing your unique perspective once you do.

YouTube is too good of a chance for a business owner to pass up. It's a platform you should use because of the volume of traffic, search engine visibility, and enthusiastic customers. Individuals have the opportunity to create their businesses, audiences, and revenue streams. The moment has come to start creating your channel because YouTube and video, in general, are still on the rise across desktop and mobile devices.

HOW TO SET UP YOUR YOUTUBE CHANNEL

The two keys to building profitable YouTube channels are producing excellent content and using your marketing acumen. If no one is coming to watch your excellent videos, releasing them would be a complete waste of time and effort. So, don't limit your attention to creating content. Building traffic can be tiresome, but it is ultimately worthwhile. In this situation, you can pay social media marketing firms to carry out these duties on your behalf.

YOUR FRIEND IS METADATA

When launching your YouTube channel, this is by far the most crucial thing to consider. The metadata is what will distinguish your work from other stuff. Your title, keywords, description, and tags make up this. When people are looking for material, it makes it easier for them to find your videos. Since YouTube will utilize this information to rank your video, it will also aid in increasing the visibility of your material. The most effective keywords can be discovered with the use of YouTube trends.

The choice of keywords to concentrate on can also be made via social media marketing services.

DIVERSE CONTENT IS CRUCIAL

Most YouTube channels have a consistent theme, but it need not be very specific. Changing up your material will give viewers something to look forward to. As a general guideline, you want to provide material that is both timely and evergreen (pull content) (push content).

Push content focuses on videos your subscribers want to see, whereas pull material has a higher chance of going viral.

THUMBNAILS WITH BRANDS

You want to make sure that people can recognize your channel from the thumbnails shown in the search results as you start to publish more and more material. The thumbnail you want to display can either be a consistent image or use comparable formats. Regardless of what you choose, be sure it's consistent.

CONSISTENT RESOURCES

You should add continuous content to your YouTube channel. Otherwise, you risk losing the audience you first attracted. The number of subscribers a channel has is what spurs growth. As a result, pay attention to the content that attracts visitors and continuously release videos with similar themes. If you can persuade individuals to sign up for your service and keep doing so, you're doing something well.

CREATING GOOD CONTENT FOR YOUR CHANNEL

The phrase "Content is King" applies equally to videos. Each new, genuine, relatable, innovative, and interesting video that these YouTubers upload to their Channel provides viewers a sense of satisfaction and that their time was well spent. Giving the content they are releasing the utmost priority is one of the traits of successful YouTubers. They are aware of the factors contributing to the subscriber list's expansion, and they handle their responsibility sensibly by producing compelling content.

These YouTubers also stick to the focus of their Channel and only post content that does the Channel complete justice. This is the secret to retaining current subscribers, increasing views, grabbing the interest of new audiences, and ultimately bringing in new subscribers.

Almost all successful YouTubers follow a timetable to post their videos on YouTube constantly. The number of videos they can post in a week or a month is unimportant. It depends on how frequently the videos are posted. They are aware that daily video publishing serves no use if it does not benefit their viewers. Of course, quality is more important than quantity. It's critical to know how quickly you can make the videos.

Although making a video may seem easy, it requires some work. To create the ideal video, one must first have a brilliant idea, then translate that idea into a video (note the number of takes), edit the video, and so on. They can now clearly see how regularly they can produce videos. The YouTubers then inform their viewers/subscribers of the frequency of their video postings, either in their introductory video or in the channel description. This makes it plain to the audience when to look out for a video. Successful YouTubers live up to the expectations once they commit.

You've probably all experienced this at least once while viewing YouTube videos; some information that can be given in a minute is extended into an eternal, imprecise video. What a waste of time and an annoyance for the audience. This is not a method of restraining audiences. Unless there is a need for more explanation, how-to/DIY videos, beauty tutorials, tips & tricks, and other similar content should get straight to the point. Successful YouTubers specifically keep this in mind when producing videos. Their video will benefit the audience, whether in entertainment, education, or other benefits.

Stick to your topic and keep your emphasis there if you're serious about starting your own YouTube channel. Before choosing a specialty, you should first determine your areas of passion. Second, how successfully can you inform or amuse viewers in that market? Will you be able to succeed in the selected niche, thirdly? How certain are you that a subscriber who first joined your Channel out of a desire to play the guitar would stick around once they start seeing videos about how to train pets? How probable is it that the other subscribers will experience that? Unless he is a pet lover interested in learning about it, that means one less subscriber for your Channel. The key to success for top YouTubers is their excellent habit of remaining devoted to their subject. Sticking to the specialty benefits YouTubers and viewers since they can more effectively target their audiences (they can choose to subscribe if the niche falls in their interest zone).

INTERACTING WITH YOUR VIEWERS AND YOUTUBERS ALIKE

When we interact with our communities, YouTube LOVES US. The more involvement we receive, the better we must be, and YouTube raises our rating in both Google and YouTube's search results.

Nobody outside of YouTube is entirely aware of how its algorithms operate. Still, I believe it's a pretty safe bet to say that not all forms of involvement are equally valuable. For instance, a remark is for one point, a subscriber's comment is worth two points, a video answer we make on our channel in reaction to our material is worth one point, a like is worth ten points, and a video response from another channel is worth fifty points.

I'll be the first to say that these numbers are purely conjecture, but there will certainly be some weighting mechanism, and video reactions from one channel to another will be quite high on that list. Additionally, I predict that since YouTube values involvement so highly, acceptors of video responses will be given more weight than the video posted in response.

If I'm right, it means that the person who accepts the responses will benefit from the exchange just as much (if not more) as the person who wrote the response.

We should enjoy the interaction as YouTube does. I'll also take a look at another factor, altruism.

Altruism generally refers to the idea of helping someone out without expecting anything in return. Since humans get a high when helping others, I've always maintained that there is no "true" altruism.

Let's say that my understanding of how YouTube considers interaction is completely incorrect. Don't you think that helping someone else is generally a wonderful thing to do? Don't you feel good about it?

In all seriousness, if you believe that by approving a video answer, you run the danger of someone unsubscribing from your channel, you have very little faith in the caliber of your content, and that's what you should be focusing on!

Simply enough, video responses boost engagement for both the poster AND the recipient.

Six Youtube Interaction Strategies

I often consider YouTube more of a social network than a place to store videos because of the amazing discussions and interactions between video creators and their fans.

I've seen some YouTube creators interact with their viewers in the following six inventive ways:

1. **Request feedback or suggestions from the audience**

Since Epic Rap Battles have asked their fans, "who won? Who's next?" in every episode for years, you've probably already noticed this and requested that they choose "who's next!"

2. **Produce videos in response to viewer requests.**

In the Screenjunkies program "Honest Trailers," the producers create videos based on fan suggestions for episodes that receive the most requests.

3. **Reply to feedback on your videos.**

My favorite example is always Mike from the PBS Ideachannel, who does an amazing job of generating discussion around his videos by responding to every comment.

4. Identify specific viewers by name

Wouldn't it be wonderful if one of your favorite actors from your favorite program suddenly turned to the camera and called YOU out? If your name is Lisa N and your favorite celebrities are Glove and Boots, then this is what's happening:

5. Include user-generated content in your videos.

Give your followers some attention; they may be among the most creative individuals on the planet. Whether they are producing fan art, song covers, reaction videos, or even their channels, they deserve some recognition.

6. Invite the audience to join the show!

Your followers are actual individuals, not just statistics! You can socialize with them just like you can with other actual people.

DOS AND DON'TS FOR YOUTUBE VIDEO REACTIONS

- Make sure it is in some manner pertinent.

- Send the channel owner a brief message outlining why you believe their reaction is appropriate.
- Make sure to show that you have read their information and that your response is appropriate (this may be obvious in the video title)
- Do suggest that they feel free to leave comments on your channel.
- Avoid spamming everyone. Nobody enjoys spam.
- Avoid spamming individuals with video replies.
- If your replies aren't considered, don't become upset or discouraged.

HOW TO SHOOT AND PICK YOUR IDEAL CAMERA

The size of video cameras has decreased, while tape formats have changed from analog to DV and HD to 4K, with matching improvements in quality and usability. There is now a larger—some could even say "bewilderingly wide"—choice of cameras available. The primary categories are detailed in the list below:

1. Specific camcorder

The dependable dedicated camcorder, which was once the only means to record video, is now only one among numerous options. Benefits include a classic design for comfortable shooting, specific settings and functions for videomaking, and a broad zoom range on a single integrated lens, as demonstrated by the Panasonic HD camcorder.

It is also made to take a range of add-ons, like a handheld rig, an external microphone, or an on-camera light. The drawback of camcorders is that they cannot record wide-angle views. While the majority can capture a wide field of view, they can hardly fit all the subjects in a room into the frame. Making videos is its only goal, which presents another problem. Because they can't use a camcorder to send a text or make a phone call, some users might pass one up.

2. Digital SLR

When it comes to still photography, nobody does it better than the digital single-lens reflex camera, or digital SLR for short. Still, it turns out that many models can also record HD video at a respectable quality. This is fantastic since it allows for higher-quality recording because the image sensor is substantially larger than traditional camcorders.

The camera can use any lens that fits its mount, allowing you to record videos with lenses ranging from ultrawide to extremely telephoto. Additionally, you may use still images to create a video that includes an audio track and perhaps some music. Numerous attachments include mounting rigs, extra microphones, and LED illumination.

On the downside, the camera's settings and ergonomics still make shooting easier than videomaking, and accessories can be pricey.

3. GoPro

This miniature miracle is tough, waterproof, and reasonably priced. It can be mounted on almost anything to capture stunning quality, from the rider's perspective on a BMX bike to a unique perspective on a skydiving helmet, as demonstrated. Even 4K footage, the newest ultra-high definition television standard, can be recorded by some models. The GoPro can only take pictures from an ultrawide angle, which is a drawback.

4. Smartphone

A few years ago, using a cellphone to record a serious video would have caused you to roll your eyes because the quality of the footage was frequently poor. No longer, since important works like the Oscar-winning documentary Waiting for Sugarman have been recorded on the phone. The audio and video quality can't be changed, which is a drawback. There aren't many options for accessories either.

5. Webcam

In the extremely improbable event that your computer does not already have one, a webcam is affordable to buy. It is, therefore, ideal for circumstances where you sit in front of a computer. Sit down, assess the lighting, and begin speaking. You're good to go because most cameras can now record in HD. The drawback is that you must remain still or risk moving out of the picture. If an external microphone is not being used, the audio may sound "thin." Furthermore, you may appear awful if the lighting is too harsh.

Three easy camera settings that will simplify life for every YouTuber

Many things catch you off guard when you launch a YouTube account. One of them was the overwhelming amount of stuff I had to remember when it came to videoing my a-roll, at least for me (the bit when you talk to yourself while staring at a lens).

But with practice, I've become so proficient at videoing a-rolls that I hardly even have to think about anything other than priming my memory cards and pressing the record button.

Three camera settings are all that matter and shouldn't ever stand in the way of you recording your next video.

1. **Select the proper recording settings and file format.**

Various recording formats are available for your camera, whether a DSLR or a smartphone. Those who delight in pixel peeping and ensuring every last bit of color is taken into account will all have strange names (often acronyms) that mean nothing to most of us.

I don't belong to that group. I also won't say they waste their time because I respect their enthusiasm.

But there isn't much time to fuss with file formats when regularly videoing yourself for a YouTube channel. Therefore, you must first choose a format and stick with it consistently (or, at least, until you buy a new camera).

The suggested file format option for your camera can be found on YouTube. I always act in this manner. Finding experts who can advise on the appropriate format for editing speed and image quality (there is always a balance) is the trick.

The file format may also include a setting for the color depth (often stated in [number]-bit), a recording setting (typically a number and letter combination such as "100m"), and the frame rate, depending on the sort of camera you're using. Search YouTube once more for camera-related content; you won't need to do this again.

2. **Autofocus**

Again, this will depend on the camera you're using, but if it's a recent DSLR or a contemporary smartphone, autofocus will be present in some way.

The autofocus on smartphones is excellent. It works, so you don't need to worry about it. So, if it applies to you, skip stepping three.

However, if you're using a DSLR, explore the autofocus options. It should be possible to use eye or face tracking; if so, activate it. If not, try something else if it's offered.

You're on to something good if your camera's autofocus consistently keeps your face, especially your eyes, in sharp focus as you move around the frame. Place it and forget it.

If your camera's autofocus is excruciatingly slow or completely unreliable, you must choose manual focusing before each video.

3. **Predict your shutter speed, ISO, and aperture, then forget it (for a roll)**

These are the three most crucial camera settings you may use, and you might need to adjust ISO and aperture quite frequently.

However, today's topic is a-roll video making, which refers to the actions you'll take in front of the camera. You shouldn't ever need to adjust these parameters if your a-roll is shot in a fixed location that uses artificial light.

You will undoubtedly want to adjust the ISO and aperture occasionally if you also shoot a b-roll (for example, product shots). If so, write down the a-roll settings so you can remember them later.

However, if you typically sit or stand in the same place and have your lighting equipment, you shouldn't need to adjust these settings for an a-roll.

For all three settings, consider these brief tips:

The one setting you should never have to modify is shutter speed. According to the usual rule of thumb, your shutter speed should be twice as fast as your frame rate (or there or thereabouts). Thus, setting your shutter speed to 1/50 is the ideal choice if you're shooting at 24FPS.

Your camera's ISO setting controls how sensitive the sensor is to light. The image will be brighter but noisier the higher the number (although this is less of an issue on newer cameras). If you want to be well-lit without being overexposed, set yours as low as feasible (or at the base ISO the manufacturer suggests).

Aperture: This determines how much of your background will be blurry, or "bokeh," in your photographs. The more blur you see behind you, the lower the number. Set the bokeh to anything you choose because it is purely a creative decision. Remember that the aperture will affect your image's brightness, so you might need to balance this setting with the ISO.

Once you've perfected your image, leave the settings above in place or note them if you anticipate making any changes while videoing the b-roll.

Camera settings should be the last thing you mind while shooting an a-roll. You must use this essential YouTuber tool to your advantage, which simply entails pressing the record button and acting naturally. That effectiveness can only be attained with straightforward, dependable camera settings that don't require frequent adjustment.

THE BEST TOOLS TO GROW AND MAKE MONEY FROM YOUR YOUTUBE CHANNEL

YouTube is open to anyone. Growing your YouTube subscriber base and making money is difficult. You must be patient and create quality content for 6-8 months before seeing results.

To grow your channel faster, understand your audience's needs, optimize your content for keywords, have a solid marketing strategy, and test monetization modes.

There are great tools to help you do all that.

In this chapter, I'll share the best YouTube tools for growing, managing, and monetizing video content.

BEST YOUTUBE SEO & YOUTUBE ANALYTICS TOOLS

YouTube is the world's largest video streaming platform and second largest search engine, where millions of people search each month.

Use YouTube SEO to optimize your videos for the right keywords to attract viewers and subscribers.

Here are the best YouTube SEO and analytics tools.

1. TubeBuddy

TubeBuddy is a popular YouTube content optimization and keyword research tool.

It's a Chrome extension that lets you research YouTube's most popular topics and keywords.

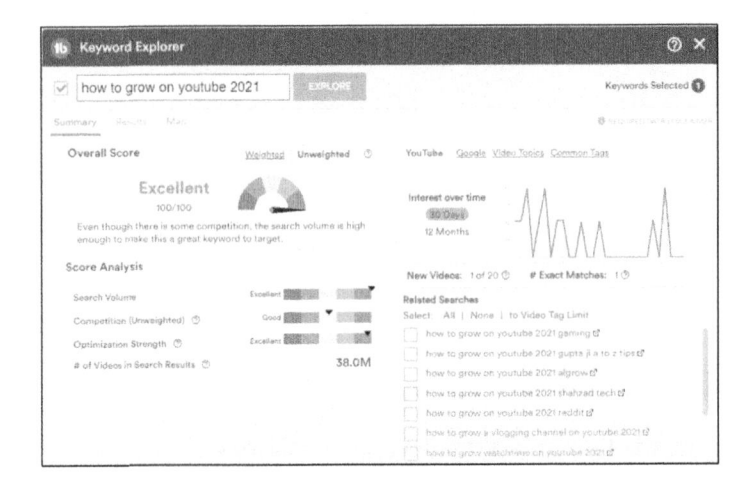

It helps you test video thumbnails to find the most engaging.

TubeBuddy helps with YouTube SEO, keywords, publishing, and scheduling. It lets you create and store video cards. Title, description, tags, etc., can be scheduled.

2. **SEMRush**

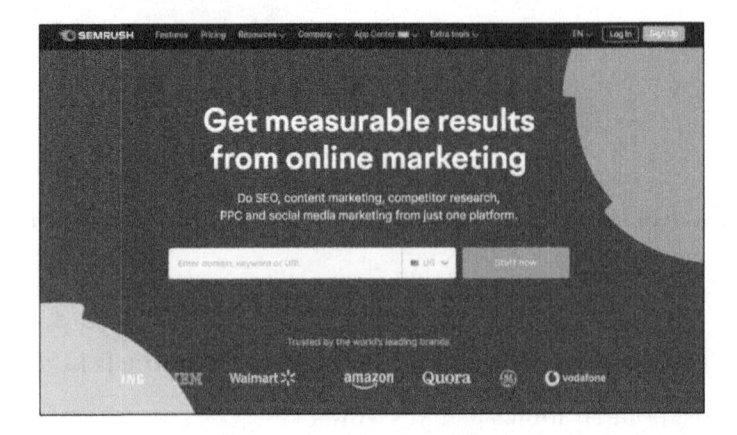

SEMRush is a top SEO and keyword tool that helps users find profitable keywords.

You can use it to find out about your competitors, do keyword research, and get ideas for YouTube videos.

The Keyword Magic Tool from SEMRush can help you find the long-tail keywords that send traffic to your competitors.

Google and YouTube keyword search volumes differ. Google-popular keywords are also popular on YouTube.

3. **Tubics**

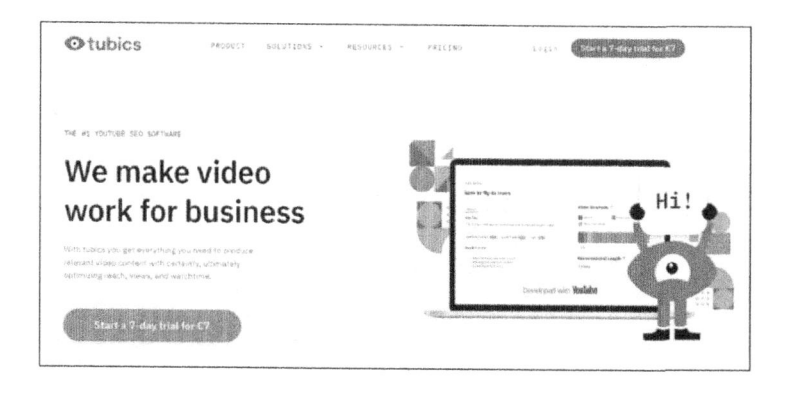

Tubics is a one-stop YouTube SEO solution that removes the guesswork from video marketing.

It optimizes content throughout the marketing funnel. You can use it to find YouTube video ideas and high-traffic keywords.

Tubics also audits and optimizes YouTube videos. Tubics evaluates your videos and makes search optimization recommendations.

It also finds the best video length, thumbnail, transcription, etc. It's a YouTube research optimization suite that helps you create winning content.

4. VidIQ

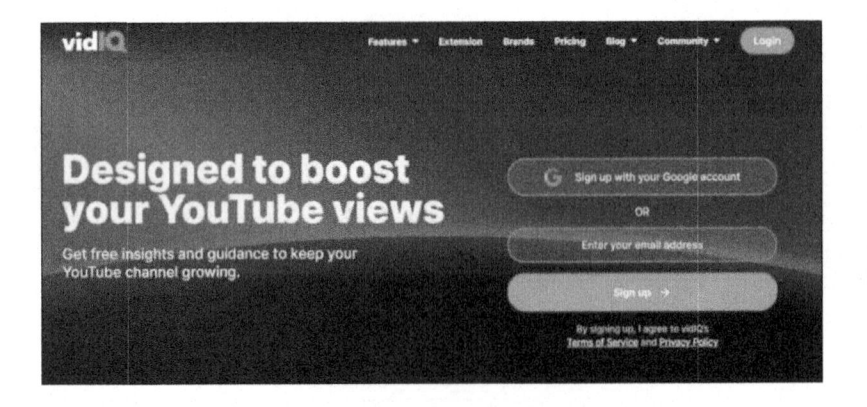

VidIQ is another YouTube content optimization and research tool that boosts reach and engagement.

It has mini tools for YouTube keyword research, title and description optimization, competitor analysis, channel audit, and trend analysis.

VidIQ helps you find profitable YouTube content ideas and keywords to optimize video titles, descriptions, tags, and transcripts. Its A.I. idea generator is a great source of engaging content ideas.

VidIQ also has a thumbnail generator and a scorecard to measure video optimization.

5. **Keywords Everywhere**

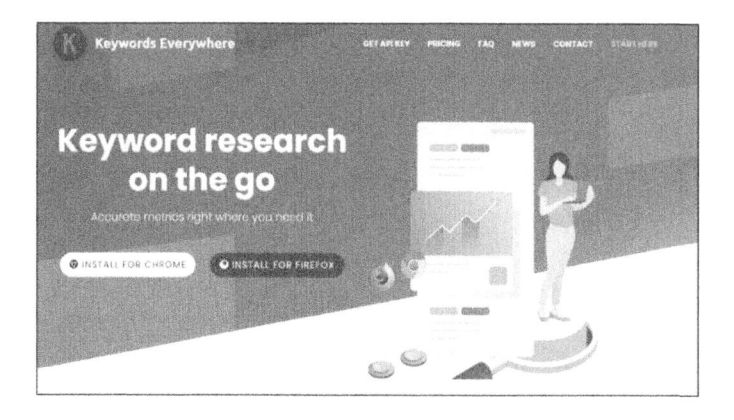

Keywords Everywhere help you find YouTube video topics and keywords.

Once installed, it shows YouTube keywords as you browse. Keywords Everywhere show you related keywords, keyword search trends, the most popular channel, average video views, and more when you search YouTube for "weight loss tips."

Keywords Everywhere show you a video's tags and related tags to optimize YouTube videos.

You can get free keyword lists but subscribe to a premium plan to get search volumes and other data.

BEST YOUTUBE MONETIZATION TOOLS

Once your channel gets regular views and subscribers, you can monetize it.

1. Izea

Izea is the world's leading influencer marketing platform, connecting YouTubers with brands.

As a content creator, you can use Izea to promote brands that resonate with your audience and make money.

Izea's smart platform matches YouTubers with brands. This is important because you can feature relevant brand products in your content. Such content helps brands.

2. Uscreen

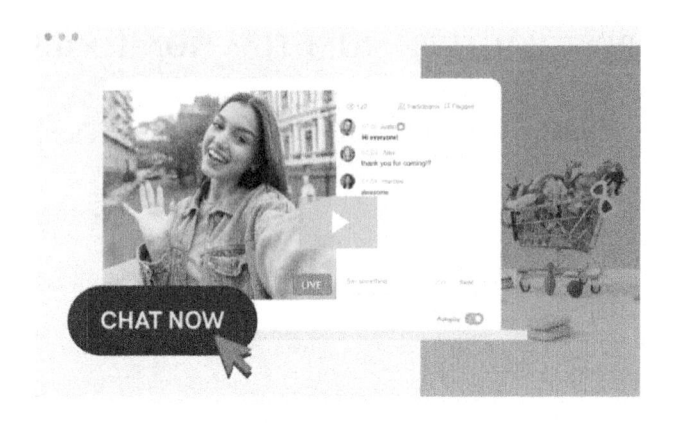

Uscreen is a video membership platform that converts YouTube viewers into paying subscribers.

You create a Uscreen premium membership site with exclusive video content and charge subscribers.

Uscreen lets you charge viewers in various ways for premium content. Uscreen subscribers pay to watch videos. Or sell a subscription or video bundle. Lifetime memberships and limited-time content access are also options.

Uscreen offers landing pages, opt-in boxes, and other conversion tools to convert YouTube viewers into paying subscribers.

3. **Patreon**

Patreon is the world's leading membership platform for creative professionals to get paid for their work.

As a YouTube creator, use Patreon to create members-only content for your subscribers. You can offer on-demand content, behind-the-scenes videos, and fan-created videos.

As YouTube's monetization policies tightened, Patreon's popularity soared. Some of YouTube's most popular channels charge for Patreon access and make more money than ads.

You'll use YouTube's growth to fund Patreon. It's a better way to monetize video content.

BEST YOUTUBE LEAD GENERATION TOOLS

YouTube creators can generate leads to grow their businesses and subscriber base. Building a subscriber base outside of YouTube is important in case YouTube suspends your channel.

1. GetResponse

GetResponse is an email marketing, lead generation, and landing page builder. Even non-technical YouTube creators can build landing pages and generate leads with this tool.

GetResponse can help you increase YouTube subscribers and generate leads. It provides ready-to-use landing page templates, so no design is needed.

Just enter your content, add a lead magnet, and publish.

Lead generation:

You can promote your opt-in offer at the beginning and end of your videos and in the description.

You can use GetResponse's email automation features to send different email sequences to subscribers and turn them into customers.

2. Kajabi

Thinkific is similar to Kajabi. It also has email automation, segmentation, and landing page-building tools for online course creators.

Kajabi is a great choice for generating online course leads from YouTube.

Its page builder lets you create landing pages quickly (no technical design skills needed). Your landing page can also host your lead magnet and opt-in forms.

Kajabi is an email marketing tool. You can set up email sequences and sales funnels to convert subscribers into customers.

You can direct YouTube traffic to your Kajabi landing page. Kajabi takes over.

BEST YOUTUBE LIVE STREAMING TOOLS

YouTube live streaming has limitations. You can't stream on multiple platforms, add effects, etc.

Several high-quality YouTube live streaming apps let you create multi-platform live streams.

1. StreamYard

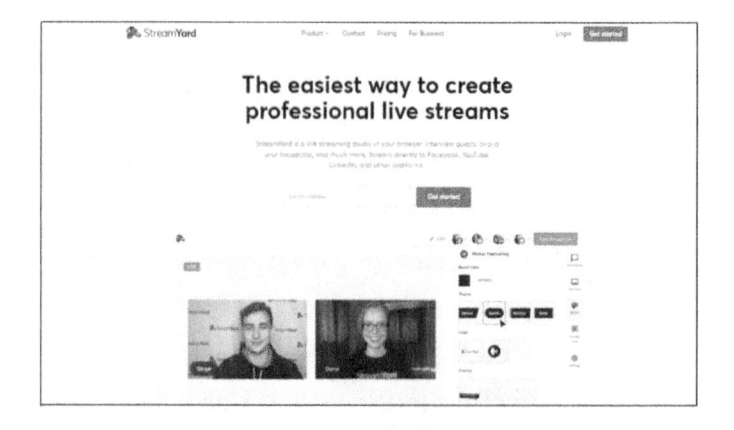

StreamYard is a top live-streaming tool. It's a web-based multi-platform streaming service that lets you broadcast live videos to YouTube, Facebook, LinkedIn, Twitter, etc.

StreamYard lets you host up to ten on-screen guests, add graphic cards with names and logos, and more. You can make your audience feel special by featuring their comments and photos on-screen.

StreamYard works in your browser; no app or software is needed. Its drag-and-drop visual editor is designed for non-technical users.

StreamYard is great for creating H.D. streams that engage viewers and drive action.

2. Open Broadcast Studio (OBS)

Open Broadcast Studio (OBS) is a free, open-source video recording and live streaming tool.

You can go live on YouTube or stream pre-recorded videos. It lets you add custom introductions and graphical elements to YouTube live streams. It gives you a unique stream key for YouTube Studio.

OBS is a free live-streaming tool that works on Windows, Mac, and Linux.

3. Onestream

Onestream simplifies YouTube and multichannel live streaming. Onestream lets you schedule pre-recorded streams, go live on multiple channels, and create professional video content.

You can live-stream video playlists on YouTube and embed your stream player on multiple sites.

Onestream's ease of use, stream quality, and professional-looking visuals stand out.

BEST YOUTUBE VIDEO EDITING TOOLS

People rarely create high-quality videos in one go. Instead, they use various editing tools and software to polish their content, remove unnecessary frames, and make their videos more presentable.

Here are some of the best YouTube editing tools.

1. Adobe Premiere Pro

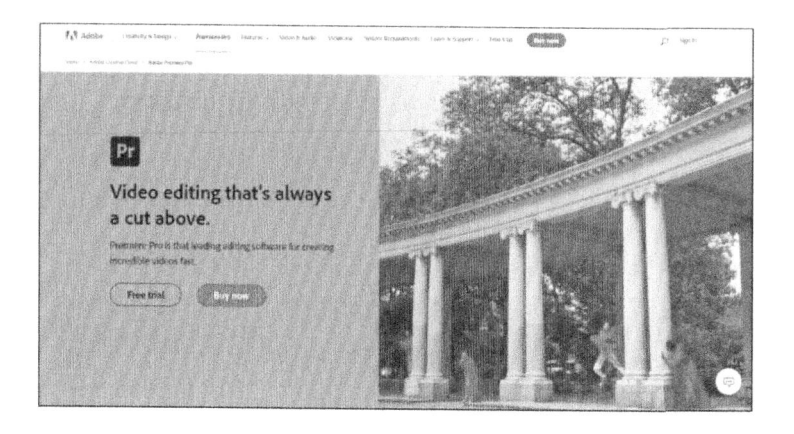

Adobe Premiere Pro is a video editing solution for YouTubers and video creators.

The ultimate video editing tool covers most aspects of content editing and transforms raw footage into professional videos.

Adobe Premiere Pro adds animated titles, transitions, and visuals to videos. Using its template library, you can import effects, color themes, sound effects, etc.

Its audio editor lets you add multiple tracks, manage volume levels, trim clips, add effects, and filter.

Its video editor can remove backgrounds, change lighting, and apply color filters.

Adobe Premiere Pro is a great video editing program.

2. Filmora

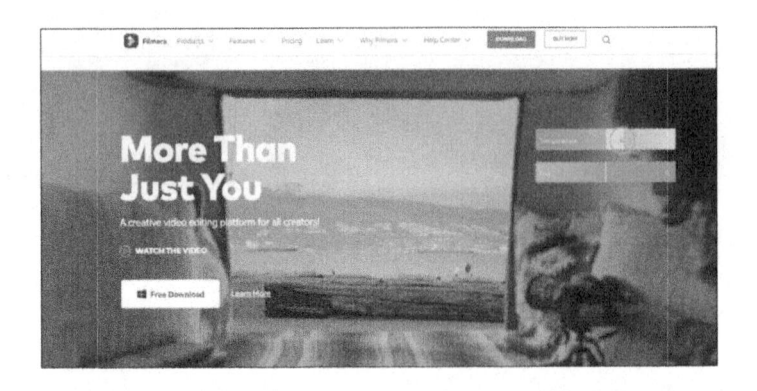

Filmora is a YouTube video editor. It's user-friendly and works on desktop and mobile.

You can remove backgrounds, apply green screen effects, add transitions, trim and cut videos, and add multilayer audio.

Filmora's latest version includes text-to-speech and speech-to-text features to speed up content creation and make videos more engaging.

3. Veed.io

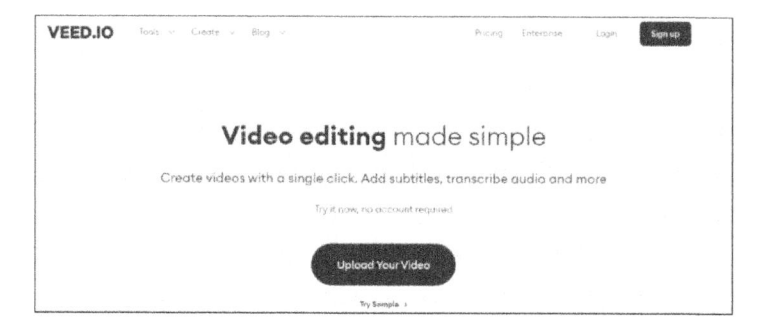

Veed.io streamlines video editing. It's a powerful video editor with a drag-and-drop interface that lets you edit videos easily.

You can add images, your logo, transcribe videos, and more. It has video cutting, trimming, and multilayer audio editing.

Tips for Boosting Video Quality

To produce a professional-looking video, ensure enough light when taking your footage. The finest lighting for a video will be the soft light in the morning or the evening. Use sunlight if you don't have a professional softbox.

A cluttered backdrop might ruin your video and divert viewers' attention away from you or your subject. A wall or plain backdrop paper is best for a "sit and talk" video.

Relevance of audio: Most viewers can tolerate the video's blurry images, but they will stop watching as soon as they hear a dreadful sound. Therefore, the first piece of equipment you should get is a good microphone.

Another factor that could cause a consumer to hit the return button while viewing your video is shaky footage. You can use a tripod or steady your camera on a surface to capture videos.

Another essential step in producing a polished YouTube video is picking a suitable video editing tool with an easy-to-use interface and a wealth of useful functions. Please pick the top video editing program from the list above.

Font: The YouTube video thumbnail is essential to draw people in and get them to watch your full video. The striking fonts are useful for it.

Learn from YouTubers who Create Video

Watching experienced YouTubers is another technique to pick up the skills necessary to produce high-quality videos. Cinecom.net, Justin Odisho, Kai W, RocketStock, and Peter McKinnon are among the ten finest YouTube video-making channels.

Create a collection of videos with similar aesthetics.

Making a beautiful video thumbnail is one of the best methods to make your video stand out on YouTube. It must be attractive, pertinent, and of the highest caliber. What the video is about should be shown in the thumbnail.

Additionally, creating a series of videos on the same subject can help you get more views and, consequently, more money from advertising. Add a number to the thumbnail to make it easier for your audience to decide which video to watch next.

You can use a safe online editor like Fotor to make a video thumbnail for one video or a whole series of videos. You can utilize and edit a sizable selection of their contemporary, lovely Video thumbnail templates in under a minute.

Make a good first impression to captivate your audience and communicate your call to action. Additionally, Fotor enables you to design the ideal YouTube channel cover. A stunning cover like this can entice viewers to subscribe to your Channel.

BEST YOUTUBE ROYALTY-FREE CONTENT TOOLS

Images, videos, sound effects, and music help make videos memorable and high-quality. YouTube's Audio Library has hundreds of sounds and tracks.

Here are the best royalty-free content platforms for YouTube videos.

1. Epidemic Sound

Epidemic Sound is one of the largest YouTube sound libraries. Its soundtracks have unique YouTube track ids.

Epidemic Sound integrates with your YouTube channel to provide a list of audio tracks.

Epidemic Soundtracks are pre-screened and approved by YouTube, so you don't have to worry about copyright claims or takedowns.

2. Shutterstock

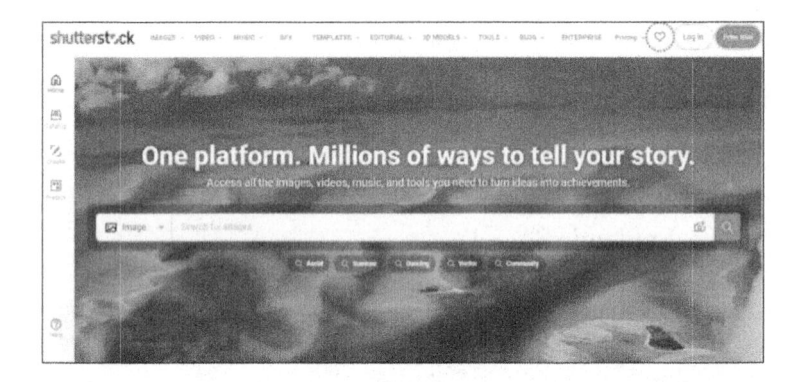

Shutterstock is the largest collection of stock images, videos, soundtracks, etc. Pay for visuals for all content categories to use in YouTube videos.

Shutterstock's strength is content quality and variety. Shutterstock lets you try images before buying to choose the best ones for your content.

If you're a professional YouTuber who needs stock photos and videos, Shutterstock is your best bet.

BEST YOUTUBE CONTENT MANAGEMENT TOOLS

Growing your YouTube channel requires proper content management, scheduling, and promotion.

Here are my favorite YouTube tools.

1. Hootsuite

Hootsuite lets you plan and schedule YouTube videos.

It helps you identify your content's highest engagement time and provides other actionable insights to improve its performance.

2. Trello

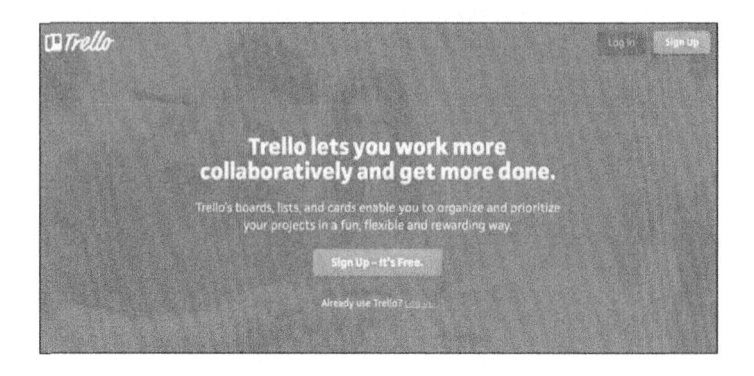

Trello is a user-friendly project management tool Youtube creators can use to organize their video ideas and streamline content execution.

It uses the Kanban methodology, where you can divide your video creation process into steps such as idea generation, script design, storyboard, content creation, editing, and publishing.

You can create separate Trello cards (dedicated threads) for every project and organize them under each category depending on its position in the production cycle.

It's an easy way to visualize your content creation process, organize your thoughts, and streamline communication across your production team.

Which YouTube Tools Are Best?

I've shared multiple YouTube tools in every category to help you.

These products offer free trials or plans. I recommend you shortlist the most relevant ones from this chapter and take them for a trial run before making the final choice.

HOW TO UPLOAD A VIDEO TO YOUTUBE, STEP BY STEP

In addition to being the most widely used video-sharing website worldwide, YouTube is the second most visited website. YouTube marketing is worthwhile your time, regardless of whether you want to increase the marketing efforts of your small business or have an online blog and want to promote your free website.

Creating a YouTube channel and adding videos to it is rather easy. Before publishing your video:

Verify that YouTube will play your video file.

Make sure the platform supports your video format before you can successfully publish your video to YouTube. Fortunately, most file formats are supported since YouTube is a video-only platform. The complete list is available here:

- .MOV
- .MPEG4
- .MP4
- .AVI
- .WMV

- .MPEG-PS
- .FLV
- 3GPP
- WebM
- DNxHR
- ProRes
- CineForm
- HEVC (h265)

You will need to export your video file type again using a supported format if it isn't included in the list above. For assistance with conversion, you may also use YouTube's troubleshooter.

A guide to YouTube video uploading

1. Enter your YouTube login information.
2. Next to your user icon, messages, apps, and notifications click the video icon in the upper right corner of the window.
3. Then select "Upload a Video."
4. Once you've located the video file saved on your computer, click "Select files." You might also simply drag and drop it into the window.

5. Post your video now. Additionally, you have the option of scheduling your post.

Include information like privacy settings, thumbnail stills, and SEO data to ensure your video performs at its best.

Choose your privacy preferences.

Your video's privacy settings let you decide who may and cannot view it. The following options are available on YouTube throughout the uploading process:

Public: Your video will appear in YouTube search results and be accessible to everyone. This is the default setting, and you should make your videos public if you plan to use YouTube to sell your company or increase your audience.

Unlisted: Videos that aren't listed are still accessible to the public, but you'll have to give viewers a direct URL to access the video. Neither your video stream nor the YouTube search results will contain these videos. Unlisted videos can be used for marketing to advertise special offers or events.

Private: You alone have access to the view.

Click "Save" after choosing your preferred choice.

Improve the SEO of your video.

By clearly expressing your video's content, YouTube SEO increases the likelihood of your video appearing in both Google and YouTube search results.

Use a tool like Google Keyword Planner or Wordstream to conduct keyword research to get going. This aids in identifying the pertinent search terms and expressions your target audience uses. They'll be more inclined to watch your video if it appears in search results this way.

When it's time to submit your video, change the file name, file description, and title to reflect the keywords you've chosen.

Additional information

Audio: After uploading your video, you can edit the audio track with music and sound effects from YouTube's extensive (and free) audio library.

Blur faces: From the "Enhancements" tab, blur the faces of anyone who appears in your video. The 'Custom Blur' option gives you additional control over the setting.

End screens: Include an end screen in your video's final 5–20 seconds that displays links, subscribe buttons, playlists, and other content. To make the procedure simpler, you can even use templates.

Cards: Cards can display personalized pictures, headings, and calls to action while directing users to a specified link (from a list of acceptable websites).

Closed captions are simple to include in videos thanks to YouTube: Just choose the language and add a file. You can use transcription to have YouTube automatically sync the spoken portions of your video for more accurate captions.

Select a thumbnail. The image viewers see when navigating through your feed is your video thumbnail. Ensure your image is crystal clear, accurately represents your video, and encourages clicks.

Once your video has been successfully uploaded to YouTube, it can now be found by other people. To increase the number of views, share the link on social media and with your family, friends, and acquaintances. You might eventually earn money on YouTube as you increase the popularity of your Channel. However, you can also promote yourself if you want to succeed as a YouTuber.

Make sure to perform the following to keep both your website and YouTube channel updated and looking good:

To add a recently published YouTube video or playlist to your website, use a tool like Wix Video.

Create quick videos you can embed on your website with Wix's video maker, then use Wix Video to submit them directly to YouTube.

To automatically add new videos to your website, sync your website with your YouTube channel.

THE IDEAL SIZE AND DIMENSIONS FOR YOUTUBE VIDEOS

Every YouTube creator knows the necessity of staying current with the platform's constantly evolving video requirements, particularly the Youtube video size.

You already know that YouTube is the king of online video and a safe bet, whether you use it for hosting or running ads. The platform constantly adds new updates and features, which have new requirements, to maintain its top ranking. You must know the proper Youtube video size to ensure that your video is properly displayed (and appears more frequently on Google).

However, rearranging the Internet to meet the updated social media standards can be tiresome. Fortunately, we have you covered.

Why It's Important to Use the Recommended YouTube Video Size

Making Youtube videos has never been simpler, thanks to our digital age, especially when you have top-notch tools like Lumen5. But if you ask any well-known YouTuber, they'll all tell you the same thing: you need to choose the right YouTube video size to maximize your chances on the site (i.e., to get more views and earn more money).

There is a lot of rivalry in the nerd era when marketers depend more than ever on video content. Ensuring your material is top-notch and adapting your video to each platform can help you stay relevant and succeed.

Let's look at the revised and accurate YouTube video size without further ado.

How Big Should a YouTube Video Be?

On YouTube, a wide variety of video formats are available. Use the following dimensions to obtain the greatest quality and prevent problems (such as video cropping):

- YouTube's HD video resolution cap is 1280 x 720 p
- YouTube video resolution HD 854 x 480 480p minimum
- 360p in standard definition at 640x360
- YouTube video size minimum: 426 x 240 240p for conventional websites

Other crucial YouTube video specifications to remember are:

File size cap: 128GB

Video length cap: 12 hours

The following video formats are supported by YouTube:.mov,.mpeg,.mp4,.avi,.wmv,.mpegps,.flv, webM, and 3GPP

YouTube policies: suggested upload encoding options

For your videos, YouTube suggests using the following encoding settings:

- MP4 container
- No Edit Lists (or the video might not get processed correctly)
- front of the file with moov atom (Fast Start)
- Codec for audio: AAC-LC
- Stereo or Stereo Plus 5.1 channels; sample rate: 96 or 48 kHz
- Codec for video: H.264
- Continuous scan (no interlacing)
- Top Notch

- next two B frames
- GOP closed. GOP of one frame per second.
- CABAC
- varying bitrate No bitrate cap is necessary.

Subsampling for colors: Frame rate: 4:2:0

It is recommended to encode and upload content at the same frame rate as when it was captured. There are several common frame rates: 24, 25, 30, 48, 50, and 60 frames per second (other frame rates are also acceptable).

Before uploading, interlaced content needs to be deinterlaced. For instance, converting footage from 1080i60 to 1080p30 requires going from 60 interlaced fields per second to 30 progressive frames per second.

How to Correctly Use the Resolution and Aspect Ratios of YouTube Videos

On a desktop, YouTube's default aspect ratio is 16:9.

The player will "automatically frame them to ensure that they are displayed correctly, without cropping or stretching, regardless of the size of the video or player" if you upload videos with a different aspect ratio.

YouTube will "add padding for optimal viewing" for different aspect ratios, such as 9:16 (vertical videos on desktop browsers). When using the Dark theme, the padding is dark gray by default.

Don't directly add padding or black bars to your video for the best effects; instead, let YouTube handle it and offer the optimum watching experience.

YouTube Video Size: Recommended Techniques

The best YouTube video size for a typical video is 1080p or 1920 x 1080, according to marketing expert Kristen McCabe from G2. "1080p will offer you that polished appearance while consuming less of the data on your phone while uploading videos. Because, let's face it, data is valuable to all of us. Nobody wants to go quickly.

Additionally, "using 2K or 4K on your phone will quickly run out of space," she continues.

720p YouTube video resolution will work for customers who are still experimenting with their Channel and want to maximize storage capacity, according to Kristen. Even while watching on big screens like LCD monitors, 720p will still give your viewers the High Definition experience they want.

Remember that YouTube encourages users to upload videos that are "as close to the original, high-quality source format as possible" at all times.

How to Change the Size of a Youtube Video

Watching videos in a higher or lower resolution is simple on Youtube. This is the procedure.

- Visit your YouTube video and select "Settings."
- youtube-video-settings
- Click on "Quality" at quality-youtube-video.
- Use this link to select the YouTube video resolution that you want.

It's over; you're done.

HOW TO MAKE YOUTUBE SHORTS

YouTube Shorts are short, vertical videos uploaded from the YouTube app to YouTube, like Stories. These 15-60 second videos entertain audiences and drive brand engagement.

Using YouTube's built-in creation tools, you can capture, edit, and add music from major labels (including Sony, Universal, and Warner), add animated text, and edit multiple 15-second video clips to create Shorts.

Your Shorts viewers can share, comment, like, dislike, and subscribe while watching. YouTube content remains, unlike Instagram Stories and Snapchat.

YouTube Shorts: Why?

YouTube Shorts debuted in India on September 14, 2020, and in the U.S. on March 18, 2021. On July 12, 2021, Shorts was released in beta to 100 countries.

YouTube's V.P. of Product Management describes Shorts as "a new short-form video experience for creators and artists who want to shoot short, catchy videos using nothing but their mobile phones."

YouTube's short-form videos are similar to TikTok, Instagram Reels, Instagram Stories, Snapchat Spotlight, Twitter Fleets, and LinkedIn Stories (RIP).

YouTube has short-form videos. The first upload was 18 seconds.

YouTube Shorts is a must-have for brands and creators because it converts viewers into subscribers.

You can create a separate YouTube Shorts channel or add the widget to your main channel. Keep Shorts on your main channel. Aligning your YouTube main feed and Shorts content will make it easier for your audience to engage with your videos and subscribe to your channel.

Your Shorts are accessible via the YouTube app's Shorts tab.

94

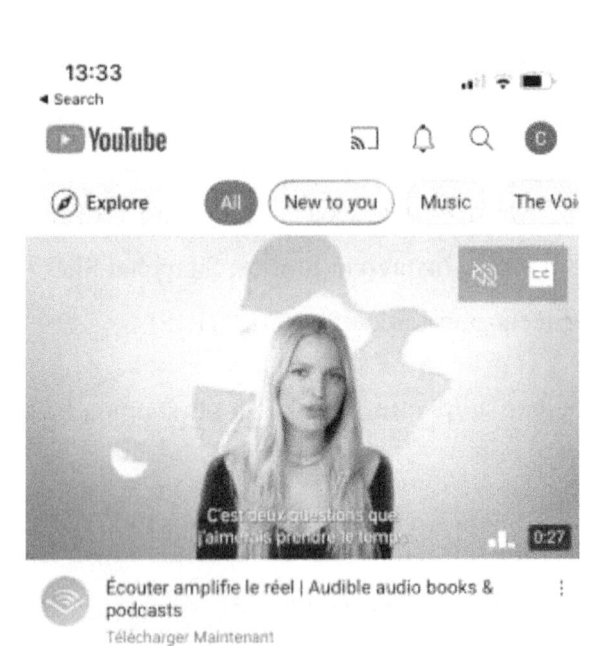

YouTube Shorts length?

YouTube Shorts are 60-second vertical videos. Shorts can be 60 seconds or 15 seconds each.

Using YouTube music limits your Short to 15 seconds.

YouTube automatically labels 60-second videos as Shorts.

HOW TO MAKE AND UPLOAD YOUTUBE SHORTS

1. **Download YouTube first.**

Only the YouTube app supports Shorts. YouTube is smart to keep everything in one place rather than requiring users to download another app to create Shorts.

How to access YouTube:

- Search YouTube in your app store (iOS or Google Play).
- YouTube app download
- Google or YouTube logins work.

2. **Create a YouTube short**

- Tap the (+) icon on the app homepage, then Create a Short.

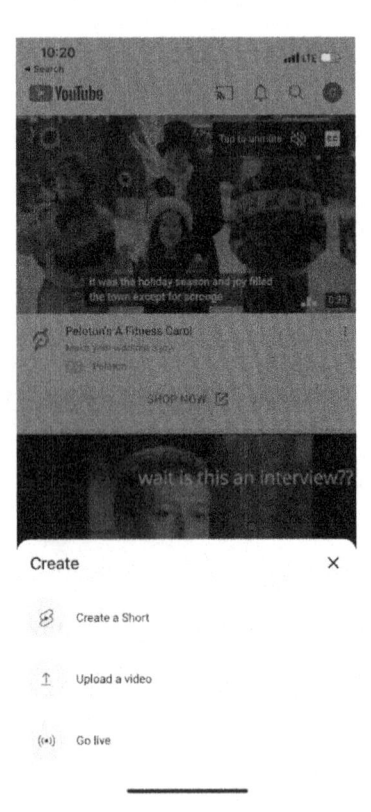

- Hold the red record button or tap it to start recording and again to stop.
- Tap 15 above the record button to record a 60-second video.

- Use the right-hand toolbar to add special effects to your video.
- Tap rotating arrows to change the camera view
- Tap 1x to speed up or slow down your Short.
- Tap the clock icon to create hands-free videos.
- Tap the three circles icon to add filters to your Short.
- Tap the magic wand to retouch your video.
- Tap the person icon to add a green screen or photo from your phone's library.
- Tap the ghost icon to align video transitions.
- Tap the Add sound icon to add sound to your Short. You can only add an audio track before or after recording.

- Mistake? Tap the reverse arrow to undo.

3. **Upload your Short**

Tap the checkmark to save your Short.

Add music, text, and filters to finish your Short.

Tap the timeline icon to edit text on the video timeline.

Tap Next when done editing.

Add your Short's details and choose public, unlisted, or private.

Choose if your video is kid-friendly or needs an age limit.

Upload your video using Upload Short.

YOUTUBE SHORTS MONETIZATION

How can a business or creator monetize YouTube Shorts? Many creators and brands monetize YouTube. YouTube is the only platform that offers revenue-sharing (so far).

Good news: this wasn't always true. Shorts creators can join YouTube's Partner Program in 2023 and earn ad revenue.

To join the Partner Program, shorts creators need 10 million views in the past 90 days. Once in the program, creators earn 45% of video ad revenue.

YouTube's Partner Program is a good reason to upload short-form videos. If you can build an audience, you could make a lot of money.

BEST YOUTUBE SHORTS TIPS

- **Start immediately**

Grab the audience's attention in the first few seconds of your video.

- **Be quick**

Shorts aren't full-length videos and work best when broken up. Instead, use cuts and edits to engage your audience.

- **Playbacks**

Consider how your short will sound when looped.

- **Value-add**

Create with purpose. Instead, give your audience value through your Short and align the content with a goal, such as increasing engagement by 10% or gaining 1,000 subscribers.

- **Your hook?**

What brings back viewers? Consider how to hook viewers on your Shorts.

- **Feel good**

Long videos don't belong in YouTube Shorts. Like Instagram Reels and TikTok, Shorts is for short, snappy content like viral trends or behind-the-scenes looks.

USES OF YOUTUBE SHORTS

YouTube Shorts is ideal for reaching consumers with shorter attention spans, growing subscribers, and showcasing your brand's authenticity.

Create! 40% of businesses use short-form videos to promote their product or service. You may fall behind if you wait.

Boost your channel

Promote your regular channel with YouTube Shorts. Every time you post a Short, your content gets a chance to get a view, which could lead to a channel subscriber or engaged viewer.

When you post a Short, the subscriber box is always visible, making it easy to subscribe.

Shorts help you navigate YouTube's algorithm by increasing engagement, a key ranking factor. This should boost channel views.

Show raw video

Every YouTube video you make doesn't need to be perfect. Behind-the-scenes (BTS) video footage shows your audience your channel, brand, and products or services.

Behind-the-scenes footage can vary. Some ideas:

- Event planning
- Debuts
- Soon-to-be-released products
- Office renovations
- BTS videos establish your brand as authentic (a plus for Gen-Z) and deepen consumer trust. Showing your brand's human side with BTS is a great way to connect with potential customers, subscribers, and viewers.

Audience tease

Use Shorts to whet the appetites of potential leads. You could post a 30-second Short about an upcoming product release with a CTA to drive viewers to a longer YouTube video with more details and a landing page for early access.

Engage quickly

YouTube Shorts lets viewers engage with your brand without watching a full-length video. Because 5% of viewers stop watching videos after one minute, short-form content ensures that your audience watches until the end, receives your message, and engages with your CTA.

Trend-watch

In 2021, the K-pop group BTS partnered with YouTube to announce the Permission to Dance Challenge and invited fans to record a 15-second version of their latest hit song.

YouTube's global head of music, Lyor Cohen, said, "We're humbled to partner with them [BTS] on the 'Permission to Dance' challenge on YouTube Shorts, helping to spread happiness and build lasting connections among their fans."

Shorts allow brands and creators to jump on social media trends, such as a dance move or challenge. Keeping up with video trends will position your brand as current and increase your chances of going viral.

Improve UGC

YouTube Shorts are a simple way to request user-generated content (UGC) because anyone with a smartphone can create them. Send your new product to brand loyalists and ask them to create YouTube Shorts showcasing the unboxing experience to expand your brand reach.

Cost-cutting

Cost-effective video marketing strategy: YouTube Shorts. Anyone with a smartphone can create the format, eliminating the need for a creative agency or video marketing company.

YouTube Shorts should be part of your social video strategy, not the whole thing. Always have a purpose for your video, and work with your social and content teams to incorporate Shorts into campaigns. To retain and delight customers, encourage YouTube subscriptions and engagement.

HOW TO LIVE STREAM ON YOUTUBE

80% of consumers prefer live videos to blog posts. 70% of users prefer YouTube Live over other live-streaming platforms. YouTube live streaming can transform your online marketing strategy.

This guide explains how to live stream on YouTube properly. I'll also share methods, strategies, tips, and tools to help you create YouTube live streams that drive more conversions.

YOUTUBE LIVE:

YouTube Live is a free live-streaming platform that lets you reach unlimited viewers worldwide.

YouTube Live is the second most popular live-streaming platform after Twitch. YouTube Live is used for live-streaming sports & entertainment events, online courses, webinars, news, and talk shows.

You can subscribe to a YouTube Live channel to watch live streams.

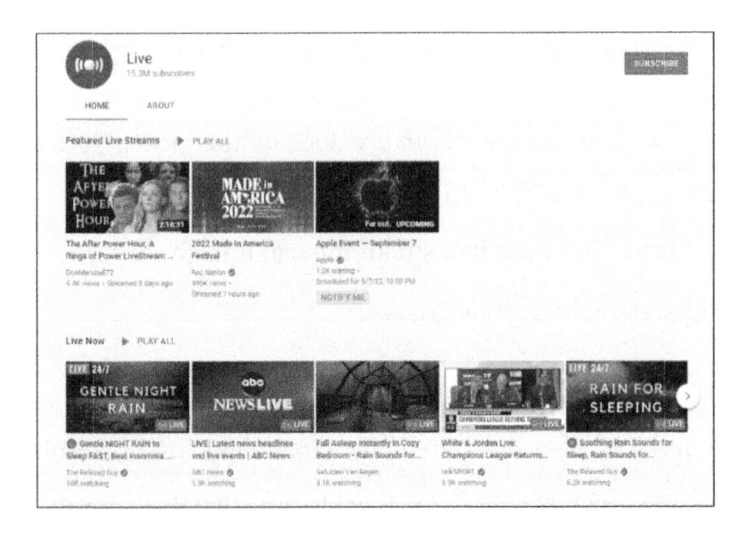

As a creator, you can make YouTube live streams public. You could also create private or unlisted live streams for selected viewers.

Once you go live on YouTube, viewers will see the "Live" icon in your video player.

They can see how many people watch your stream and comment in real-time.

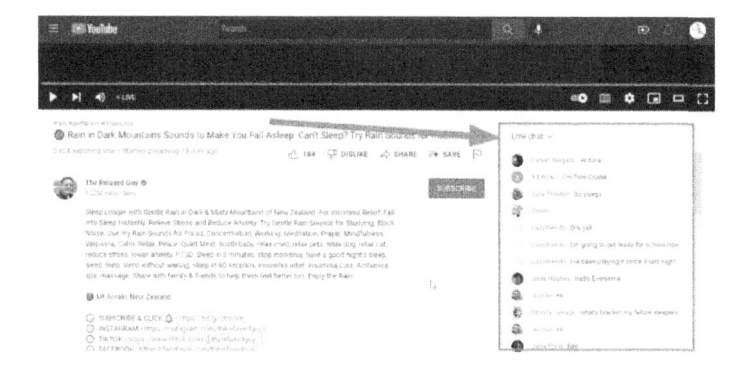

YouTube Live is so easy to use and accessible that even beginners can use it effectively.

Digital product sellers, course creators, coaches, and marketers regularly stream on YouTube.

Digital product sellers and online marketers can build their brand's credibility by showcasing their best content live during live stream sessions.

YOUTUBE LIVE-STREAMING BENEFITS

YouTube Live benefits online marketers, digital product sellers, and businesses looking to engage their audience.

Let's briefly list the benefits.

YouTube is the world's largest online video streaming platform, with 2.5 billion monthly active users.

OBERLO — Most Popular Channel Among US Digital Video Viewers

90% of US digital video viewers use YouTube, the most popular channel for digital video consumption.

(eMarketer, 2019)

YouTube Live gives you free access to millions of industry-relevant users. No other streaming platform offers free publicity.

Audience-Friendly

YouTube is the most popular app for viewing digital content on smartphones. Your audience doesn't need extra apps to watch your content.

YouTube's algorithms recommend videos, live streams, and channels based on user interests. This helps your audience find and subscribe to your YouTube channel.

Community-building

YouTube is a great place to build your brand's online audience. People subscribe to your YouTube channel when you regularly Livestream high-quality videos. This grows your online community and brand's influence.

Organic SEO traffic

Live streaming on YouTube can boost organic traffic. How? Google owns YouTube and shows relevant videos in search results.

Your live stream is added to your video library when it ends. Optimizing your YouTube video will appear in Google's search results and attract organic visitors.

Multiple revenue streams

YouTube live streaming gives your business monetization options. You can earn with Google Ads, sponsored content, affiliate offers, etc., as your YouTube audience grows. Since YouTube has the largest audience, any monetization method will likely earn you more money.

Creates partnerships

Anyone can watch your YouTube videos. As your channel audience grows, industry brands and businesses notice you. This opens up new partnership opportunities to do something unique and profitable for your business. YouTube's size and reach make such opportunities more common.

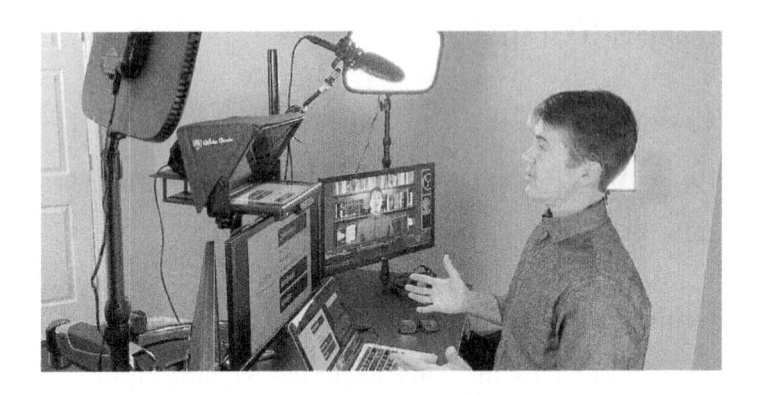

Learning Revolution founder Jeff Cobb using OBS

YOUTUBE LIVE STREAMING ESSENTIALS

Do you need any extra gear to start? True. Here are the three requirements for YouTube live streaming.

Verified YouTube

Livestreaming requires a YouTube channel. Verify your channel to use YouTube Live. This isn't YouTube's celebrity channel verification. YouTube Live only requires your phone number.

Camera

You'll need a good camera to live stream your surroundings or face. Use your phone or laptop's webcam. YouTube has no quality restrictions, but you should stream in 720p or 1080p to ensure clarity.

Microphone

Smartphones and webcams have built-in mics. You'll need an external mic if you're shooting outdoors or in a room with echo.

Encoder

Smartphone livestreams don't need an encoder. If you want to live stream your computer screen, apply visual effects, or live stream pre-recorded videos, you'll need a third-party video encoder (like OBS).

YouTube Live Streaming Options

YouTube Live offers three ways to live stream. Let's delve deeper.

YouTube on mobile

Any smartphone with an internet connection and the YouTube app can stream YouTube Live videos. Smartphones are great for live-streaming vlogs, events, and other content on the go. Live YouTube streaming is the most popular method.

To use YouTube live streaming on your phone, you need 50 subscribers. After that, you can enable limited live streaming.

You must have 1000 subscribers and follow YouTube's guidelines to access YouTube Live's full features.

YouTube Live Webcam

You can live stream YouTube content from your desktop with a webcam. Desktop YouTube Live streaming has no subscriber limit, unlike smartphone streaming. After creating and verifying your YouTube channel, you can stream content.

Desktop live streaming is ideal for online courses, coaching sessions, and presentations.

You'll need a professional external webcam for high-quality video (unless your laptop already has an internal H.D. camera).

Encoder-based YouTube live-streaming

You can stream from your phone, desktop, or a third-party encoder.

A live streaming encoder lets you share your desktop screen, add visual effects (animation & transitions), run pre-recorded videos, live stream playlists, etc.

YouTube Live encoder: why? Because it offers features not available when streaming directly from YouTube Live.

Live-streaming video games, interactive workshops, formal presentations, etc.

OBS is a popular free video encoder for beginners and low-budget content creators. Premium live streaming tools can create more polished YouTube Live streams.

YOUTUBE LIVE STREAMING STEPS

Let's discuss YouTube live streaming step-by-step.

1. **Create a YouTube account.**

Create a channel after logging into YouTube.

How-to:

- Click your profile picture at the top.
- Click Channel.
- Enter the channel name, description, and photo.
- Create.
2. You can now upload videos to YouTube.

YouTube Live is not yet available.

3. Live-stream

New YouTube channels must verify their phone number to Livestream.

How-to:

Click the camera icon.

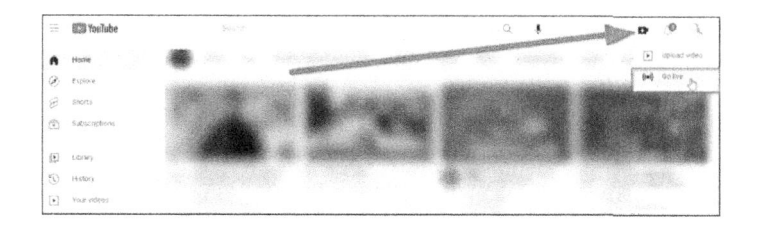

Click "Go live."

This brings up YouTube Studio with the following message.

Click Request to see the following pop-up message.

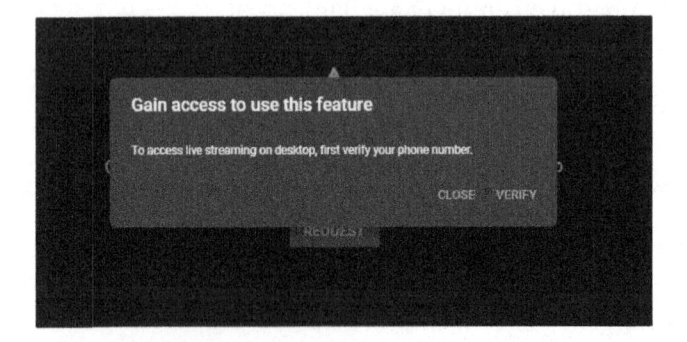

YouTube Live requires phone number verification. To verify, click Verify.

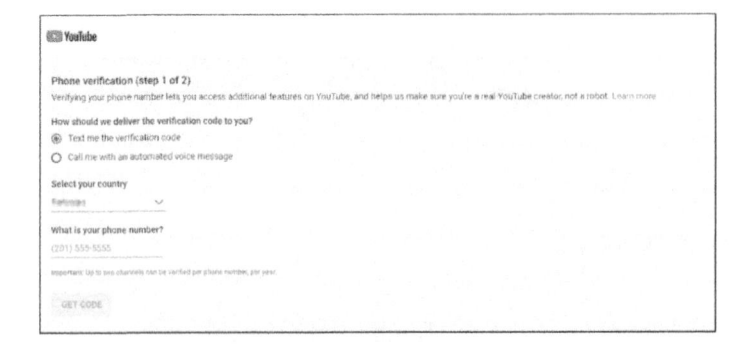

YouTube takes 24 hours to enable live streaming after verification.

When you reach 1000 subscribers, you'll get YouTube Live on your phone.

Configure YouTube Live Stream and go live

Here's how to go live on YouTube Live once your account is eligible.

Smartphone YouTube app Bottom of screen + icon.

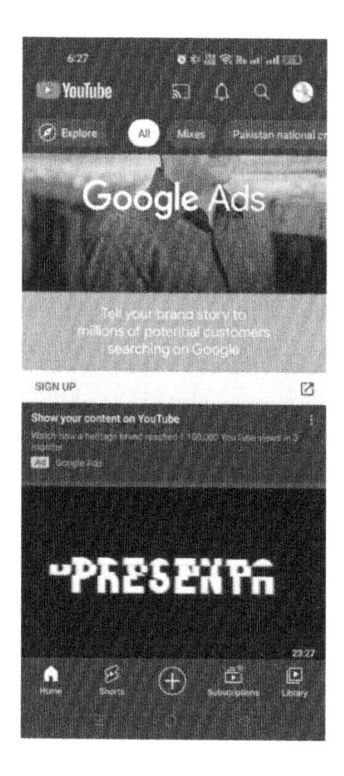

Click "Go live."

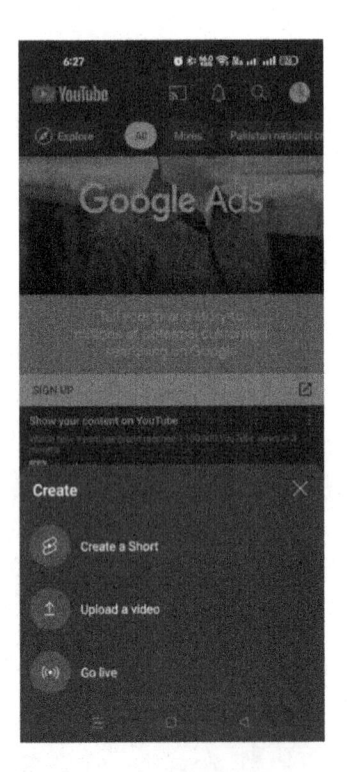

Tag your live video.

Choose a smartphone camera (front or back). This can be changed in-stream.

Choose between Public and Unlisted

Audience types (made for children or not)

Click Next when finished.

Video thumbnails (take a picture or upload an image).

LIVE!

Webcam

Sign into YouTube.com.

Click Camera and Go Live.

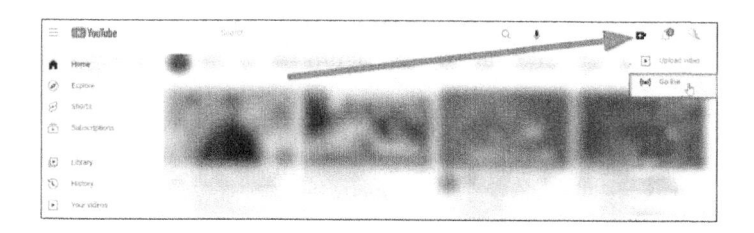

This opens YouTube Studio, where you can set up your stream. First, decide if you'll live stream now or later. "Now" wins.

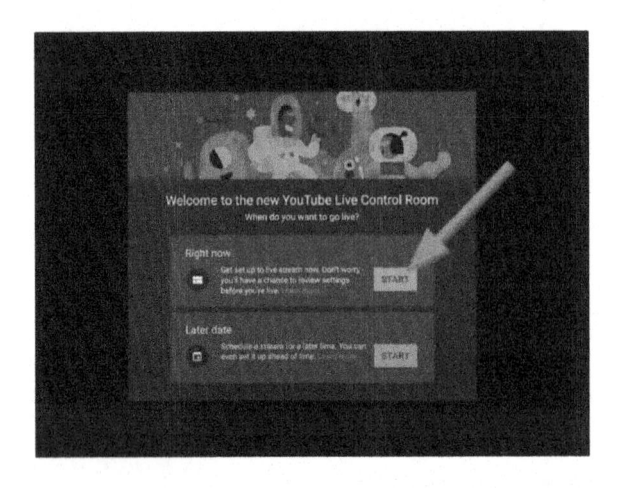

Next, choose between your webcam and a third-party streaming tool. We'll use a webcam here.

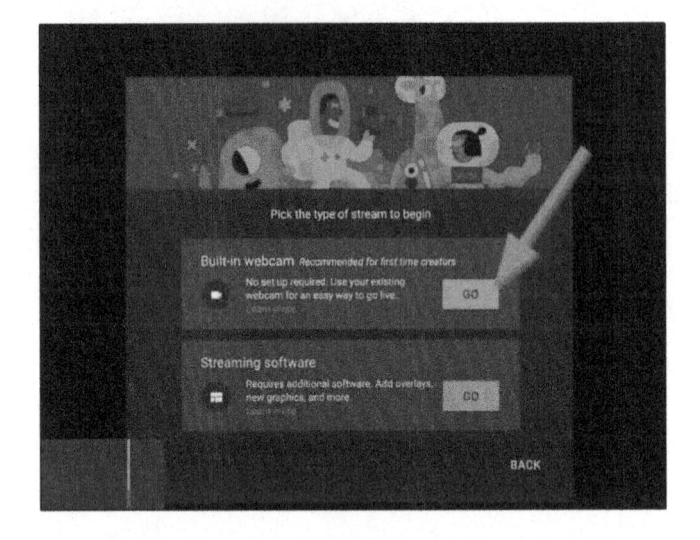

Add a title, description, and video settings. These are video stream configuration options. All configuration is self-explanatory.

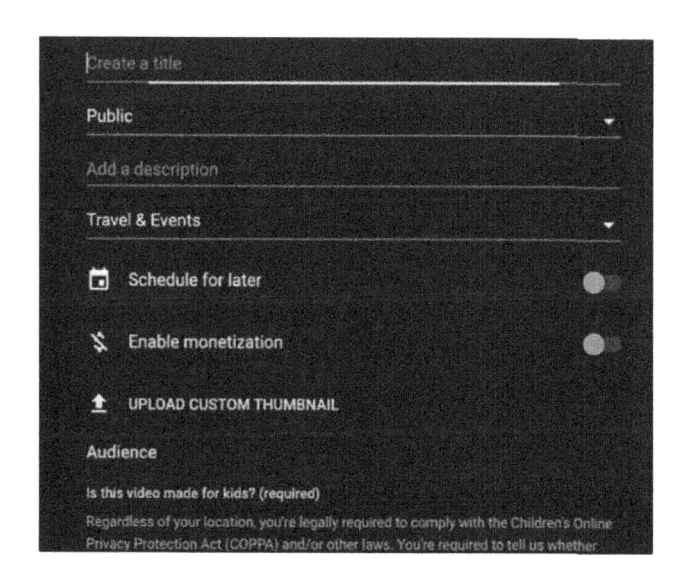

If your channel is eligible, you can also use Google Ads.

After configuring your video, choose a thumbnail by taking a photo or uploading an image.

Start streaming by clicking Live.

Encoder

Install an encoder. We'll use OBS, but you can use any live streaming tool with YouTube Live.

Sign into YouTube on your desktop and click Go live in the top-right corner.

Left-click Stream in YouTube Studio.

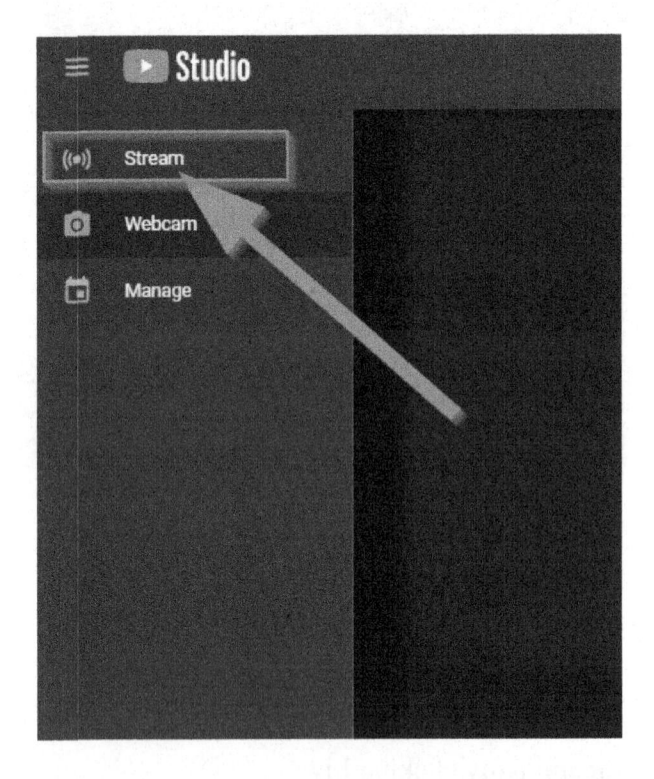

Copy your stream key from Live Studio's Stream Settings.

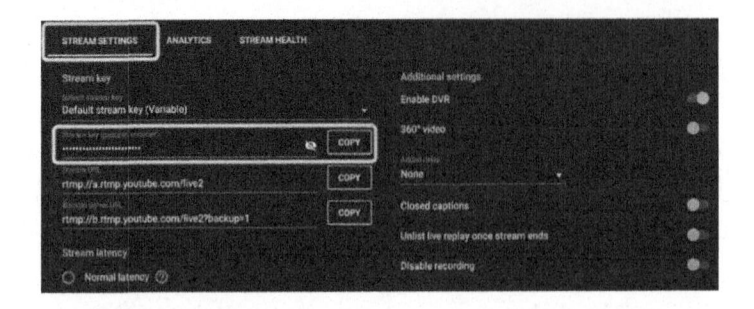

Open OBS and click Settings.

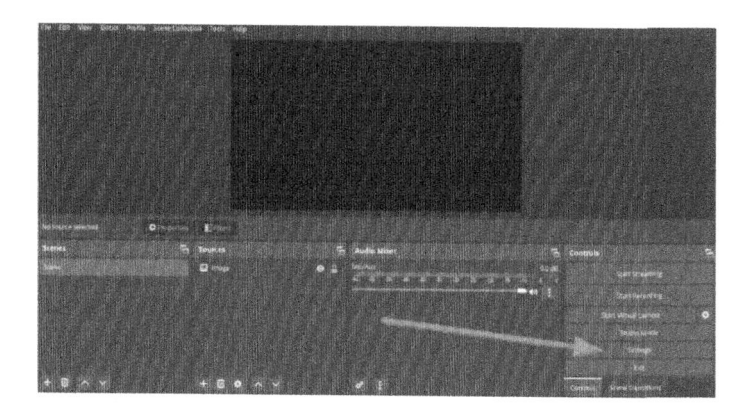

In Settings, Click Stream.

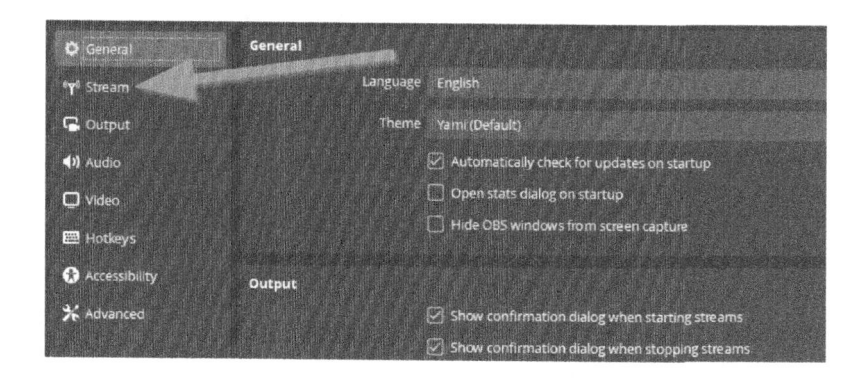

Choose YouTube from the Service dropdown.

Now click Use Stream Key to connect your account with OBS.

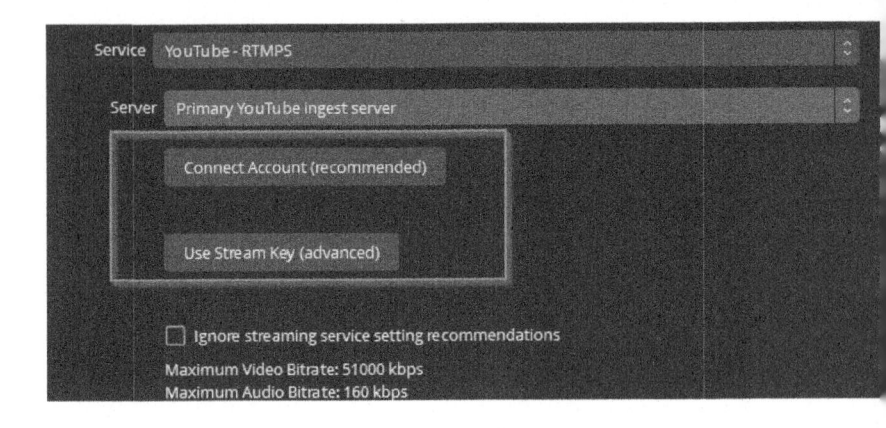

Copy/Paste the stream key from your YouTube Live Studio and click OK.

Now your YouTube account is connected with OBS.

Open OBS and click on the + icon to add a media source.

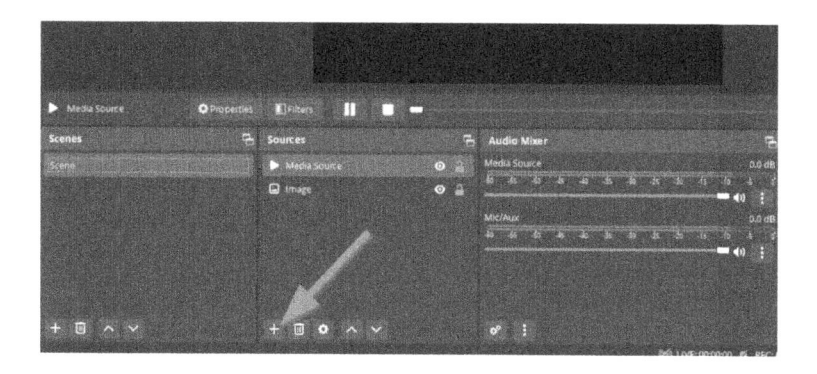

Choose the relevant media source from the menu.

Your YouTube Live channel will stream from this list. Choose "Video Capture Device" to stream from an external camera. Choose "Display Capture" for screen sharing.

Click Start Streaming to begin.

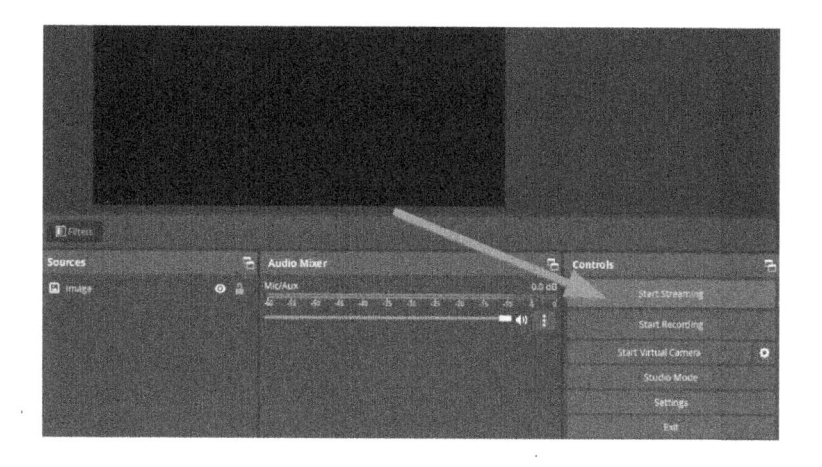

– Go back to your YouTube studio to see your connection status and Live label.

– Stop YouTube's broadcast by clicking End Stream.

– Stop streaming on OBS.

I've described connecting an encoder to YouTube Live Studio. Free OBS is limited. You can connect a premium live streaming tool to your YouTube account using your Stream Key and URL. Most tools have similar integration processes.

YOUTUBE LIVE-STREAM PROMOTION

You're excited to live stream on YouTube. How do you get viewers? I'll share some thoughts.

1. Plan your live stream

YouTube Live lets you schedule live streams in advance to build anticipation. Schedule real-time and pre-recorded live streams.

Scheduling a stream creates a premiere thumbnail for subscribers and YouTube users. Clicking the upcoming video thumbnail notifies viewers when it goes live.

YouTube recommends scheduling and announcing your stream 48 hours in advance for promotion.

2. Make a compelling trailer

Create a trailer for your upcoming live stream to build anticipation. Scheduled YouTube streams can include 3-minute trailers. Scheduled streams don't attract viewers.

You can add a trailer to a scheduled stream premiere. When someone clicks your premiere thumbnail, YouTube shows your video trailer. The same premiere broadcasts your live stream once your video goes live.

3. YouTube SEO-optimize your stream

YouTube is second to Google Search. Optimize your live stream with YouTube SEO if you want it to appear in your audience's recommended videos and drive organic search traffic. This article covers YouTube SEO basics.

4. Share

Share your live stream's link with social media and email followers. Create a YouTube post to remind subscribers of your live stream.

Ask live-stream guests to share the link to attract a larger audience.

5. Stream regularly

Regular live streams can help you grow faster. Rather than hosting a live video podcast whenever you're free, schedule it. When you follow a schedule, your audience looks forward to your content and promotes your show.

6. Live Q&As

Live YouTube Q&A sessions attract more viewers. This works well in the online course and coaching industries, where prospects have many questions.

7. Embed Stream

Embedding your live stream on your website is another good idea. If you have a high-traffic site, create a "Live Content" page where visitors can watch your live streams at set times each week.

YOUTUBE MONEY-MAKING TIPS

Ever questioned what those tiny Google ads splayed out at the bottom of some YouTube videos meant? You are not alone, though. Many people, including myself, find these advertisements annoying and choose to close the intrusive ad to focus on the video.

But why is that advertisement there? Who did that? And why is it necessary?

Before I go any further, allow me to say that for every 50 individuals who cross out the advertisement, at least one clicks on it since it appears to be a relevant advertisement conveying crucial information.

You are aware of what that implies, right? It denotes VALUE! And if, let's say, 5000 people see the video each day, that may mean roughly 100 clicks every day!

Yes, YouTube.com has begun paying creators of popular videos a portion of the advertising money that its parent firm, Google, receives from publishers. Google Ads are presented at the footer of these chosen videos.

The main difference between the previous revenue-sharing technique and the current one is that you can nearly guarantee that you will receive an email from YouTube inviting you to join the revenue-sharing program if you have a video on YouTube.com that is receiving a lot of hits, views, and comments.

This is YouTube's way of thanking and honoring you for creating a video that receives many views! And trust me when I say there is a TON of money to be made on YouTube!

You must be eager to start earning as much money as possible from your videos at this point, right?

Good, but hold on! I can't find your video! Do you currently possess a video? And who else outside your grandmother is watching your video? No? So, I assumed!

If you make a video that gets millions of views, you can rely on a steady income from the internet.

But isn't that easier said than done? How can you create a video that ranks in the top 100 videos on YouTube and brings in money simultaneously?

Getting a million views on any video you submit may not be simple, but it's no longer impossible! You can now make your YouTube video one of the top 50! All you have to do is strictly adhere to a few key tips and tricks. You can use these tactics along with the just made public YouTube insider information to:

a) Prepare a video for YouTube.com by doing the necessary research.
b) Produce a video,
c) advertise and promote it
d) monetize it!

Make Use of YouTube Video Marketing to Your Advantage!

Every single month, more than 10 million people visit the YouTube website. How could you resist wanting a piece of that pie? With YouTube video marketing, you can. It's quite simple! Here are some suggestions to help you maximize your investment.

- Use the access you will have to your visitors to your advantage. Know that every time you publish a video, it will be visible to everyone. Make your video entertaining and educational if you want to attract the attention of millions of people.

- Your chances of being viewed increase with the number of videos you have. Have you ever searched for someone and discovered that they had uploaded thousands of videos? One of the things you may do to achieve enormous success in the YouTube community is this. Posting new content as frequently as possible is a great way to enjoy YouTube video marketing.

- High-quality videos are crucial. Invest in a high-quality camera to enable you to create detailed, high-quality videos.

The secret to having your video seen is traffic. A fantastic YouTube Secret Weapon tool can show you exactly how to use unique techniques created just for YouTube to drive the most attention to each of your videos.

The future of marketing is video; when used well, it may increase your sales significantly. The newest and best method of promoting anything you sell is through YouTube videos. Start producing videos your audience will appreciate instead of doing things old-fashioned.

HOW TO MONETIZE YOUR CONTENT

Every day, a huge number of people upload videos to YouTube. Unfortunately, very few individuals are even aware that they may make money from the videos they upload to YouTube.

You may access YouTube in various ways and let it generate income for you. The vast majority of those who profit from YouTube often operate some kind of home-based business.

But there are always other ways to monetize YouTube. Your home-based business can be promoted through your videos, affiliate marketing materials, or even by selling your physical goods.

SEVEN METHODS FOR MONETIZING YOUTUBE

Let's examine each of these sources of income in more detail.

1. Be a member of the YouTube Partner Program.

The YouTube monetization scheme lets you place advertising inside your videos once you sign up as a partner. You will be compensated for every view and click on one of your commercials appearing in the video.

The requirements to join the program are quite simple: you must be at least 18 years old and not use vulgar language or promote hatred in your videos to be accepted. You may already have hundreds of YouTube videos you can immediately monetize by going into your channel settings.

Now that you have a real way to make money online, those interested in starting a YouTube channel don't have to join a home-based business or even need any advertising money or capital.

2. Selling goods or products

You can monetize your channel on YouTube by selling products to your viewers. Whether it's T-shirts, coffee mugs, tote bags, snapbacks, or anything else, merchandise can help you in more ways than just the bottom line.

Incorporating your online persona and brand into physical goods is a great way to reach a wider audience. And because your supporters can more fully "buy into" your work, you'll have a tighter bond with them. Roman Atwood, a designer, has stocked his store with a wide range of products bearing the Smile More logo.

Branded products are easier to sell than most people think. On freelance websites like Fiverr, you can find reasonably priced designs tailored to specific products, like t-shirts.

You can enjoy all the benefits of a print-on-demand business with less effort if you connect your store with order processing solutions like DSers or one of the many print-on-demand companies that handle shipping, fulfillment, and customer service.

Instead, you could team up with a merchandising network that caters to creators, such as DFTBA (Don't Forget to Be Awesome). You'll compete with other YouTubers, but you won't have as much freedom as you would with your eCommerce site in terms of adding products, offering discounts, integrating your content, and so on.

Luxy Hair, which sells hair extensions, uses YouTube to advertise the products by posting how-to video tutorials on the website.

As a YouTuber with a sizable following, you'll enjoy two immediate advantages that other business owners will find hard to match:

- A source of ongoing content that drives traffic to your shop
- The trust your audience has placed in you after you've consistently offered them your unique brand of content for free.

3. Use crowdfunding to finance your upcoming artistic endeavor.

Crowdfunding is a viable option when monetary constraints prevent an idea from being realized.

If your project's pitch is compelling enough, you can reach out to the crowdfunding community for the money you need to upgrade equipment, pay actors, or cover other production costs.

Like this popular Kickstarter for Kung Fury, a short film paying homage to '80s action movies, you might want to film a video outlining your idea or providing a taste of what it would be like.

• Kickstarter is one of the most well-known crowdfunding platforms and has a history of backing projects by YouTube creators. Popular online resource for raising money for creative projects and ideas. Don't expect to get funding unless you can prove you can bring in the money you need.

- Indiegogo. In contrast to Kickstarter, this alternative gives you a wider variety of funding options to work with.

Inspire your audience to donate by praising their support.

You can ask your fans for financial support by setting up "fan financing" channels like crowdsourcing.

You can add your voice to the internet without charging your audience for access if you're a creator. Therefore, if your content is high quality, your readers may be more inclined to stick with you.

Numerous fan-funding systems give artists a fresh audience for their work and a way to connect with and express gratitude to their most devoted supporters.

If you choose to use crowdfunding, make sure to adhere to these guidelines. Put first, make it clear how the money will be used. When your fan base cares about your story or mission, they'll start seeing the true value in your actions.

A second suggestion is to offer tempting incentives for larger donations. If you can make them feel special for being such a dedicated fans, you can expect more pledges and larger contributions.

Several well-liked methods for fan funding include:

- **The Super Chat on YouTube.** Super Chat is a tool used for YouTube live streaming. It enables you to set up a tip jar so visitors can add money anytime and as much as they want. As mentioned above, you must configure your YouTube account for advertising.

- **Channel affiliations.** Members-only benefits are available in exchange for monthly donations from viewers who support your channel. Similar to Super Chat, access to this function requires membership in YouTube's Partner Program.

- **Patreon**. This is the membership website that facilitates easy payment of creators. For as little as $1 a month, followers of their favorite creators can subscribe to gain exclusive benefits.

- **Tipeee.** With the help of this platform, you can receive both one-time and recurring donations.

- **Buy Me A Coffee.** Through Buy Me A Coffee, creators and artists can take membership fees and donations from their fans. With over 300,000 creators, it's considered the "#1 Patreon Alternative." The distinctions are that Buy Me A Coffee makes it simpler to accept contributions, that there is a flat 5 percent cost for all features (as opposed to up to 12 percent for Patreon), and that payouts are instantaneous.

4. **Permit media outlets to use your content**

If you create a potentially viral video—say, a funny one starring your dog—you may be able to recoup some of your production costs by selling the rights to the video.

If your videos gain widespread attention, producers from television news shows, morning shows, and online news websites may contact you to ask permission to use your work.

Videos can be included in a marketplace like Trusted Media Brands, making it easier for the right people to find and buy your content.

5. Work as an influencer for brands

With their typically large advertising budgets, brands are investing more and more in influencer marketing and sponsorships, paying influencers who have already earned the loyalty of their audiences.

If you can strike the right deals, this offers you, as a creator, a tremendous opportunity.

To calculate your starting flat rate, YouTube marketing guru and influencer Brendan Gahan recommends multiplying your typical number of views by $0.05 to $0.15. (which is around what many brands are willing to pay for views via YouTube ads).

The following are possible costs for influencer marketing on YouTube, per WebFX data:

- For a YouTuber with 10,000 subscribers, $200 per video
- For a YouTuber with 100,000 subscribers, $2,000 per video
- For a YouTuber with 1,000,000 subscribers, $20,000 per video

If the brand is a good fit, you might be able to negotiate higher pricing depending on your leverage, which includes your audience demographics, the caliber of your material, and how distinct and lucrative your niche is.

When working with brands to create sponsored content, it's important to be open and honest with your audience about your motivations. This includes not advocating something you don't genuinely like or believe in.

You can join your channel and be discovered by both big and small brands in the following influencer markets:

- Crowdtap. To earn money and other rewards, you must complete short "tasks" that require you to create content. In terms of fan base size, entry is not restricted.
- Upfluence. More than three million influencers can be found in this platform's database. Users can use Upfluence's keyword search to connect with producers and form partnerships.

Some influencer markets provide freebies, while others are well-known for the high prices big brands are willing to pay to be featured there. Use the resources that work best for you, but sign up everywhere you can to maximize views for your channel.

6. **Promote Affiliate Goods.**

Affiliate marketing entails endorsing a product or service made by another business to earn a commission. As an affiliate marketer, you have the opportunity to promote various brands through the use of product placements, testimonials, and other content. However, it would help if you clarified the partnerships to those who watch your videos.

This is a great strategy if you review products on your YouTube channel. Since the brand is not taking any chances, the threshold for new entrants is low (they only pay when they make sales).

Affiliate programs like ClickBank and Amazon's Affiliate Network (commissions range from 1% to 75%) are very common (up to 10 percent per sale). It is common practice for businesses in your field to operate affiliate programs in the e-commerce industry.

PART TWO: STRATEGY

THE PERFECT VIDEO RECIPE

It's easier to say than to do without committing to YouTube. You frequently experience exhaustion or confusion, especially if you always strive to maintain a strict publishing schedule. Therefore, you must have a content plan to offer you the freedom to experiment and expand your YouTube channel.

And good news for you! We're here to give you step-by-step instructions on developing a YouTube content plan that will enable you to accomplish your video development objectives.

Let's begin immediately.

1. Define your YouTube channel's goals

Setting goals for your YouTube channel should be your first step. After all, having a purpose to strive toward rather than producing content arbitrarily is one of the cornerstones of a successful content strategy.

These goals may seem to be aiming to:

- Give up your job to focus only on YouTube and establish a second source of income there.

- This year, continuously publish more high-quality videos and produce more experimental works.
- Cooperate with other YouTubers to get additional income outside of AdSense.

You should contemplate this.

- What do I hope to get from this content and my YouTube channel?
- What does success entail for my YouTube channel and me?
- How can I monetize my content in ways other than just YouTube?

To better understand your Channel's goals and how to fulfill them.

Then, establish certain criteria you must meet each year to have a timeline. Keep in mind that your goals should be attainable and practical.

2. Investigate Your Target Market

Once your objectives are set, you must know the audience you are writing for. This will enable you to create better content that aligns with your audience's preferences.

You may be asking just what information you need to know about your target market.

There are four essential things you should learn:

- **Demographics:** the gender, age, and geographic location of your audience. This will assist you in determining the language and writing style that best connects them.
- **Psychographics:** These are the characteristics, such as motivations, values, way of life, insecurities, and aspirations, that influence the behavior of your audience. (Starting with Gartner reports is a good idea.) these assist you in learning how to engage your audience emotionally.
- **Online behavior:** It refers to the kinds of media and content your target audience consumes online, the channels they subscribe to, the social media sites they use, and the amount of time they spend on each. This gives you knowledge about how to approach engaging your audience and how they interact with content online.
- **Offline behavior**: It includes your audience's purchasing patterns, routines, interests, occupations, and preferred places to spend their free time. This

can also help you understand how to engage your audience on an emotional level.

It's important to remember that practically all of these require considerable inference from your industry knowledge.

Your target audience overview can be improved over time as you learn more about your audience and how they respond to your content and gain more insight into them. Always be sure to assess your target audience's assumptions regularly.

You can also use the audience you've established on other platforms to contact them for information directly! For instance, you may survey your audience on Facebook, Twitter, and LinkedIn. The Question Sticker is also usable on Instagram.

You are set up for success if you have chosen your audience and are aware of their viewing preferences. You must begin by speculating on the audience that most connects with your content. The customer persona is then modified over time as you come to know your audience and consider what you've learned about them.

3. Examine the competition

It's time to look at what your rivals are doing now that you know what your target audience wants to see. That will provide suggestions for the kind of material you should create. Investigate rival YouTube channels in your niche to start. Investigate and make a note of what these channels are doing. This implies:

- Observe the videos the makers in your field produce (such as tutorials, long-form vs. short-form videos, etc.).
- Subscribing to competitive channels: note how often artists release new content.
- Reading the comments on rival videos will help you delve further into the comment sections. Look at how people evaluate the information published in your niche, identify the current authors' shortcomings, and note what you might improve.
- Consider the types of videos your competitors' viewers are watching and engaging with most (think of it as finding out the crowd-pleasers).
- You can start brainstorming other ideas for subjects you wish to cover in your videos when you've finished.

We advise mixing up different kinds of material, such as Response videos, live streaming, opinion videos, and how-to videos since it will keep your viewers interested and establish you as an authority in your field.

To prepare for the following step, come up with at least 20 video concept ideas.

The very best place to start is on YouTube. The more research you do on YouTube, the more prepared you'll be to succeed.

4. **Schedule Your Content You should now make a content calendar.**

This publication schedule specifies the content, release dates, and frequency of your online video content. Create a publishing calendar based on the 10 concepts you selected in Step 3.

Therefore, you can choose a day of the week (such as Thursday) and designate that day as your posting day if one of your goals is to publish more frequently, say once a week.

This is a fantastic YouTube marketing strategy that will pique the interest of your viewers in your videos. You can better organize your video content if you have a plan. On other sites, you can see which videos would make good end screens and which groups of videos can be in the same playlist.

You'll be able to point viewers to other helpful videos and keep them on your Channel longer, which will be very helpful for audience retention. Additionally, bear in mind that while having a plan is excellent, things do occasionally change.

Perhaps some business-related news has to be discussed, or you devise a better plan as the weeks' pass.

That's okay; you should be able to pivot regardless of what it is:

Because even when circumstances change, a sound strategy will keep you on course.

You should consider how each video contributes to achieving your overall objectives as part of your content marketing strategy. (Are the ones you set in Step 1 still in mind?)

In actuality, you can use many monetization techniques for every video.

For instance, if one of your objectives was to earn more money than from YouTube advertisements, you could construct a video specifically targeted at the affiliate network in which you participate.

We advise content creators to know their choices for monetizing their work. (Spoiler: Demonetization is a major issue for creators, as ad revenue is declining.) Because you'll need to look beyond video ads if you want to create content full-time.

So be sure to consider other strategies that will enable you to monetize YouTube. This may consist of the following:

- Associate connections.
- Offering tangible goods for sale.
- Offering digital products (like access to your podcast or a subscription site).
- Brand alliances.

You must be fully aware of the monetization alternatives available for your material. Don't limit yourself to AdSense earnings. Consider your alternatives before deciding what you want to do to make money from the content you are producing.

5. Execute Your Plan

It's time to put these concepts into practice now that you have a content plan! The ideal video production process is divided into the following four steps:

I. Use video thumbnails and titles with search engine optimization

Create intriguing images and titles once you've organized your themes.

Make sure you build a thumbnail and headline from the concepts you've chosen that will be intriguing enough to get a click.

This is because these are the initial opportunities for contact with your visitor; therefore, you should make the most of them by grabbing their attention.

II. Make personalized video thumbnails

You may enhance your click-through rate by using custom thumbnails. If your video thumbnail is intriguing and appealing, viewers will click on it when they see it.

Pro tip: After publishing, YouTube allows you to change the thumbnails.

As a result, creating two to three thumbnails for each of your content ideas is a good video marketing technique. As a result, you have more possibilities to test out and discover, which increases engagement.

Your thumbnail ought to include the following:

- Visually demonstrate your response to the searcher's inquiry using clear imagery.
- The basic content should be concise, catchy, and contain keywords that will help YouTube's search engine better index your video.
- Bright colors: Use colors that pop against the YouTube background to make it visually appealing, and make sure your brand's colors are used consistently.
- People are drawn to other people; therefore, whenever possible, employ faces that convey strong emotions.
- Curiosity as a component: stimulate interest in your audience without giving away too much of your message.

Ensure your brand color is consistently used against YouTube's neutral background, enhancing Uscreen's branding. Mix certain images, key phrases, and people with obvious attention-grabbing expressions.

These elements will improve the message and effectiveness of your video.

- Use video titles that contain keywords
- Make sure your video titles are clear because they are the first text your viewer will see.
- When using keywords in your titles (and video descriptions), a good place to start is to:
- Look at the tags, titles, and descriptions your content competitors use to characterize their videos.
- Recognize the issue that the searcher's video is resolving.
- Pertinent keywords for our intended audience and explain what the video is about:
- Create 6 to 8 titles for your videos, then ask your trusted advisors which ones they think are the most intriguing.

It's time for you to concentrate on your video material, so make an outline and write a script for it.

Whether you prefer outlining on paper or your computer, you need to give yourself a firm notion of the flow of the video.

This will begin you thinking about the different frames you want to create and any props you'll need before videoing.

After you outline your video, start composing the script. Even if you adjust and change things along the road, we advise doing this to make production and videoing run more smoothly and effectively.

You can skip forward to the following step if you want to create videos that work even better without a script (such as reaction videos).

III.   Create Your Video, Edit It, And Review It

It's now time to video and edits your video after all of the preparation work! You should now put everything together, fix any errors you made while recording, and prepare your video for YouTube. Just remember that it's okay to get to this stage and realize something is missing or can be done differently.

Retakes are common in the industry.

Although it might be a little frustrating, doing it right the first time is preferable to settling for mediocrity.

- Spend a lot of time editing if one of your YouTube goals is to produce more high-quality videos. During the editing process, aim to:
- Place the clips in the proper order.
- If a voice-over is required, add it and sync the video.
- Take out any extraneous video, mistakes, or strange pauses.
- Include outros or intros (but use them strategically, as these can decrease viewer retention).
- Add transitions and cuts (i.e., strategically placed B-roll, GIFs, graphics, screenshots, audio snippets).
- Using color grading, you can change the color of your video.
- To aid in information retention, use text on the screen.
- These actions will significantly improve the quality of your YouTube video and apply to just about every type of video you wish to create.
- Also important is receiving advisors' opinions on your change. You may have some sort of cabin

fever if you focus on anything for an extended period.

- It will be worth your time to take a literal break from your masterpiece and have someone else look it over.

IV. Upload to YouTube.

These three stages must be finished before publishing your video.

When you post your YouTube video, make sure to enable closed captions since you want it to be as accessible as possible (you can also add them manually in the editing step).

Watch its performance over the next 24 hours to see whether you need to call in any of your thumbnail replacements.

On YouTube, suggested or recommended videos account for 75% of views. Use the YouTube algorithm to your advantage to see your videos this way. To do this, create compelling material with eye-catching thumbnails. The first stage is the title and thumbnails.

6. **Use Different Social Networks To Repurpose Your Youtube Videos**

When you publish a new video to your YouTube channel, think about using it on your social media channels. This is a fantastic method to grow any existing communities you may have on other platforms while cross-promoting your YouTube channel and attracting more viewers to your videos.

Here's how to go about it:

- Choose your social media channel carefully; pay attention to where your rivals post content (e.g., LinkedIn, TikTok, etc.), and make sure you are there. A good place to start is Facebook or Instagram.
- Analyze your competition on social media by looking at their content, posting schedules, and interaction levels when you've located them there. This will give you a fair notion of the content that will engage your audience.
- See what's valuable or shareable from your YouTube video and consider other ways you may display it. The same concept can be presented in

several formats, such as text-based postings, brief video clips, etc. Look for reuse options.

- Don't forget to include call-to-action encouraging viewers to visit your YouTube channel in your social media posts.
- Your objective is to pique people's interest in your material to the point that they want to watch the YouTube video in its entirety.
- Everything you do to promote your material should be done genuinely in the interest of helping people.

7. **Review And Modify Your YouTube Marketing Plan**

Following the publication of your videos, you must check in on them to see how they're doing. Your best ally in this process will be YouTube analytics, which you should thoroughly examine at least twice a month.

While YouTube analytics may initially seem intimidating, the following metrics are ones you should pay attention to:

- **Impressions**: the number of times people have seen your thumbnails.

- The percentage of thumbnail impressions that resulted in views is known as the click-through rate (CTR).
- **Watch time:** the total amount of time users watched your video material.
- Average view time: the number of minutes watched on average for each selected video and time.
- Average percentage viewed: the typical proportion of a video that viewers watch each time.
- Traffic sources: how YouTube users discover your video content.

The information you receive from YouTube analytics will let you know how both your Channel as a whole and specific videos are performing, which will assist you in understanding what you need to do to meet your objectives.

ATTRACTING YOUR IDEAL AUDIENCE ON AUTOPILOT

The method of driving traffic to your videos might be straightforward or challenging. You should do a few things to spread the word about your YouTube videos if you want to increase traffic. I'll demonstrate how to get traffic to and popularize your YouTube videos in this chapter.

How to Promote and Gain Popularity for Your YouTube Videos

You should upload your videos to YouTube as soon as possible. This is essential for your success. You can gain search engine traffic for your videos when visitors enter a specific query linked to them by uploading them to YouTube. Your videos will move up the rankings the more views they receive.

For various reasons, you want to raise your YouTube search engine results. These arguments might seem self-evident, but I'll state them for conversation's sake. The popularity of your video is the primary goal of increasing your search engine results. Your video will grow more popular as more people see it and generate more traffic for you. People will start spreading your information online, and it will go viral.

The next thing you need to do is put your URL in both the video's description and the actual video. In the past, visitors to YouTube had to enter your website's address into the search bar of their computer browser. However, people may now easily view your website by clicking the direct link in your description.

This is a fantastic way to receive traffic straight from YouTube. You never know when you might wish to pull your YouTube video and use it for promotional purposes, even though people can click on the link in your description. Your website's information will still be there in the article after you remove it from YouTube, allowing you to promote your website.

Encouraging people to subscribe to your YouTube channel is the last thing you want to do. This will let people know when you upload new YouTube videos. The more subscribers you have, the more views you'll receive and visitors you'll get back to your website.

Your YouTube channel could be compared to a favorite TV program. Users will visit your videos and wait until you post something new. This fan base-building is comparable to a lead opting into your autoresponder series. You may increase your video views and the potential traffic you receive by enticing viewers to watch your content repeatedly.

Using YouTube to drive visitors is a great strategy to spread the word about your website. I continue to use it today, and it is assisting in the commercial success of my website. Think about this as you create your videos; your website could achieve the same goals with some help and direction.

6 WAYS TO INCREASE YOUTUBE VIDEO VIEWS

Own a YouTube channel yourself? If so, you might be trying to figure out how to get a lot of views. Statistics show that YouTube videos receive more than 1.5 billion daily views. One viewer stays on this platform for more than an hour on average. We advise you to follow this easy technique to expand your channel if your view numbers are too low. To learn more, keep reading.

1. Encourage current viewers to subscribe

Your current audience is the best source of video views for your future content. People will be more likely to subscribe to your channel if you provide them with value. After they subscribe, your view counts will gradually rise.

You have to ask them to subscribe to your channel on YouTube. Another excellent suggestion is to include a call to action in your videos. You could also wish to include a subscription link for better search engine positioning in your video descriptions.

2. **Discover what your audience wants to see.**

You won't acquire many views if your videos don't appeal to your audience. Therefore, you should find out what your audience wants to see by asking them. In actuality, sharing information your audience likes is a terrific strategy to increase viewership and keep their interest.

3. **Create Playlists to Maximize Your Watch Time**

YouTube's statistics show that the most popular channels on the site have a large number of playlists. These companies are aware of the value of auto-play. When the content is excellent, viewers will simply keep watching videos as they automatically begin.

4. **End screens and use cards**

You can direct users to other excellent stuff using end screens and cards. Cards function like pop-ups that appear during playback. In contrast, end screens appear once your video has finished playing.

5. Make SEO-friendly headings and descriptions

If your videos aren't easy to find, no one will be able to watch them. To make your content search engine friendly, you must adhere to the finest SEO practices. So, when writing titles and descriptions, you should consider using potential keywords. Check to see if the keywords apply to your videos.

To create a list of effective keywords for your video descriptions, use Google AdWords Keyword Planner and Google Trends.

6. Use Eye-Catching Thumbnails

More often than not, content is scanned and read. Similar to this, people peruse the list of videos on YouTube before pressing the play button. Therefore, be sure that your videos' thumbnails are engaging. Using automatically generated thumbnails is not a good idea. Use custom thumbnails as an alternative.

Thanks to their social media presence, I'm confident that most of the YouTube channels on your list of subscribed channels are theirs. Naturally, I remember how I came across a handful of them on my social media profile as recommendations and how they held my attention and persuaded me to subscribe to their YouTube channel. That is the combined power of social media and quality content. One such instance is 5-Minute Crafts, which has more than 55 million users.

Successful YouTubers know how crucial having a social media presence is to advertising their Channel on YouTube. They utilize social media tools to the fullest to reach enormous numbers of social media consumers. These YouTubers can share each of their videos on social networking sites like Facebook, Instagram, Twitter, and others, boosting the likelihood of an increase in views, which could lead to an increase in the number of subscribers.

The available simple sharing tools may spread a video like wildfire and quickly reach millions of people, which is another significant benefit of having a social media presence.

YouTubers are aware that their Channel would be worthless without their subscribers. The majority of popular YouTubers engage with their followers in various ways as a way of giving back to their enormous following. If not for every comment, at least where necessary, one of them reacts to the feedback they get on the uploaded videos. The messages left by their admirers in the videos were rarely read publicly. Another approach to engaging with the fan base is through social media. Some YouTubers use live broadcasting to interact with their social media following and respond to their queries. Others, depending on the focus of their channels, solicit feedback on what they hope to include in subsequent videos, such as crafts, recipes, product reviews, tool insights, etc. Most popular YouTubers communicate with their viewers, subscribers, and fan base through the YouTube community. This gives the viewers a sense of exclusivity and inclusion in the video community.

These activities give the audience the impression that the person behind the channel/brand is keeping an eye on them, increasing their loyalty to the brand.

Successful YouTubers create playlists for their videos to be arranged according to the growing daily volume of videos on their channels. This method of using a YouTube playlist aids viewers in discovering the information or subject matter they are most interested in. The establishment of playlists also makes it easier for viewers to click on a certain playlist and view the stream of videos without returning to the Channel, which helps YouTubers increase the number of views for their videos. Making it so that both the viewers and the YouTubers benefit from this.

Not only is having the videos structured a terrific method to keep the viewers pleased, but it also significantly improves the rankings in the video search.

GROWING YOUR AUDIENCE WITH COLLABORATION

A successful partnership can raise the number of viewers, viewership, and popularity of both participating networks. Popular YouTubers accomplish this by choosing a YouTuber in the same niche as you, reaching out to them for a collaboration, and creating a video together.

Through a more direct method, such as asking the other YouTuber to mention the other YouTuber with whom they have cooperated and their Channel in their video.

Another strategy involves vloggers switching channels for a week and only posting videos made by the other vlogger.

Secrets of YouTube Marketing

Most YouTubers are completely ignorant of what a YouTube partnership is. A YouTube partnership is a program where you collaborate with YouTube and receive some significant advantages.

Benefits of a Partnership with YouTube:

Your videos will be consistently processed and served by YouTube at a higher resolution.

You'll have access to a far more thorough Insight tool via YouTube. The Insight analytics tool may be used to optimize your current and upcoming videos so that more people will see them.

YouTube will provide you with extra protection for your work. This implies that you have the option to brand your channel with special features that partners can access alone.

YouTube will provide the chance for revenue sharing. This means that Google will place banners and adverts over your video, earning you a tiny commission for each click.

Qualifications:

- You must be free of any copyright violations. There are NO exceptions; whatever you upload is your own.
- You frequently submit videos that have thousands of views each.
- Your videos must abide by YouTube's rules and terms of service.

Guidelines for a Partnership Program:

For the YouTube Partnership program, you can apply. However, make sure that your account satisfies the requirements before applying. Apply with a high upload view count and many subscribers to assure your relationship because not everyone is accepted to be a YouTube partner. You'd have a better chance of getting accepted if you waited for YouTube to offer you the partnership program.

Insight:

The YouTube insight tool is a very effective tool to utilize for video optimization. The statistics for the video are displayed in days, months, or years. Additionally, it reveals how viewers get to your videos, who they are, where the video's hotspots are, and where they are from. If utilized properly, this tool can assist you in determining how to attract viewers to your video.

Annotations are text bubbles you can add to your video on YouTube after it has been uploaded. Including interactive commentary in your videos is a fantastic idea. Annotations can be configured to connect to other YouTube videos, channels, or search results. Additionally, you can ask anyone to annotate your videos. With the use of annotations, interactive games have been created. However, you should watch out that they don't detract from crucial video details. You can manage the bubble type and color, as well as when and where they appear in your video, to prevent that.

- You may search YouTube for people's comments using the comment search feature.
- You may find out what keywords specific audiences use using insight for audience.
- You may overlay captions and subtitles on your video with Caption Tube.

Five Easy Ways to Promote Your YouTube Videos

You would want to reach a broad audience with the videos you produce for your company if you invest a lot of time, energy, and perhaps even money into making them. You aren't just doing it for fun, after all.

Videos are a fantastic tool for brand recognition and business promotion. However, people don't automatically become visible to an audience when they click the

"Upload" button. To reach the largest audience, you must advertise your videos. It will require effort, just like everything else in your company.

Here are five ways you may market your videos to start getting the word out about your company and the ones you've produced:

1. **Connect on social media.**

Social media platforms are excellent places to advertise your videos. Use the following you already have on Facebook, Twitter, Instagram, and other platforms! You can embed your videos in status updates or tweet links to them. Make your videos "pin" on Pinterest so people can find them.

You can advertise your videos by using social bookmarking websites like StumbleUpon. Remember that self-promotion is not encouraged on these platforms, so use it carefully. Promote other blogs and videos that you find interesting to keep the playing field level.

2. **Publish an email.**

Don't undervalue your email list as a resource for advertising your videos because you worked hard to build one. Include a link to your most recent video in an email or newsletter because the folks on that list are there because they want to learn more about your company.

3. Use the company blog to spread the word.

Your blog has followers because they want to know what's new, just like your email list. Describe what to expect in your video and why viewers should watch it in a blog post. Either provide a video embed code or a link to the video after your post.

4. Advertisements on YouTube.

You can choose to use Google AdWords for Video to promote your videos if you're ready to spend the money on it (TrueView Ads). The targeted audience will see the advertising on the website. The advertisement will link viewers to your video or YouTube channel when they click it. Just like regular PPC ads, you only have to shell out cash if and when someone clicks on your ad.

5. Revert to the fundamentals.

Even though web-based advertising is receiving much attention, you shouldn't discount the tried-and-true conventional forms of advertising. Send emails, phone calls, and distribute press releases about significant videos to regional media outlets. To make your video easily accessible, include a link to it in the press release.

A large audience can easily learn about your company thanks to videos. They may help you establish a solid internet presence and expand your fan following, leading to numerous new purchases.

Don't spend all that time and effort producing excellent YouTube videos only for no one to see them. Reach out to all of those prospective viewers by taking the necessary steps to promote your content.

FOLLOW YOUTUBE TRENDS TO KEEP UP

According to Comscore, the popular social network YouTube recently topped 100 million viewers. 14.8 billion online videos have been viewed overall by internet users in just January 2009.

YouTube, which for the first time surpassed 100 million viewers, "YouTube led the growth charge, accounting for 91 percent of the incremental gain in the number of videos viewed versus December, as it surpassed 100 million viewers for the first time." accounting for 91% of the incremental increase in the number of videos viewed compared to December, according to Comscore.

With a 43 percent market share in online video viewing, Google continues to outperform the competition. Of those, 99 percent of the videos seen were on YouTube.

Internet users in the United States watched 101 videos on average per person in January 2009.

You are throwing away a lot of money if you aren't using or planning to use video to sell your business or product.

Keeping up with platform changes and knowing who to believe for the best information is one of the main problems we face as YouTube video content providers. Because the back end of YouTube is so complicated, new users often get lost while creating an account. Unless they follow the appropriate individuals, they won't even know that some of these capabilities exist.

YOUTUBE GUIDELINES FOR MONETIZING CONTENT

In most cases, advertisements are the first monetization strategy you try. If you want to make money on YouTube without making videos or as a content provider, joining the YouTube Partner Program and setting up monetization is essential.

You must be a resident of a region or country participating in the YouTube Partner Program and agree to abide by all of YouTube's monetization guidelines. With 1,000 subscribers and 4,000 annual view hours, you can apply to begin earning money from your channel.

Here's how to start making money off of YouTube:

- To start making money on YouTube, you need to sign up for the channel that pays out.
- You can access your account by selecting the gear icon in the upper right corner.
- Pick YouTube's Studio option.
- Select "Monetization" under "Other Features" on the left sidebar.

- Before proceeding, please review the YouTuber Partner Program eligibility requirements and terms and conditions.
- Sign up for a new Google AdSense account, or associate your channel with an existing one. (An AdSense account is required for financial reward.)
- Determine your monetization preferences.
- When you're done, go back to the dashboard and click "Analytics" on the left. Select Revenue from the primary tabs, then look at the Monthly Estimated Revenue graph to see how much you can expect to make on YouTube each month.

YouTube Premium: What is it?

With the help of YouTube Premium, users can view and support their preferred content producers without being interrupted by advertisements. Little will change for producers because they will continue to receive payment for videos viewed by visitors and YouTube Premium content.

For YouTube Premium, creators receive payments based on how frequently subscribers watch their material. Think of the money you make from YouTube Premium members as a second source of income to go along with the money you currently make from commercials.

Even if it's simple to set up, creating a revenue stream for yourself through YouTube Partner advertising is far from the most successful.

Why you should look for Revenue outside of adverts

Due to its recent move to be more open about platform advertising and what constitutes "advertiser-friendly" content, YouTube has faced much criticism.

In essence, many YouTube creators were concerned that their content's nature would prevent them from earning the advertising revenue necessary to sustain their channel.

Your material might not be eligible for ad revenue, according to YouTube, if it contains the following:

Sexually provocative content, such as sexual humor and partial nudity

- Violence, such as severe injury demonstrations and activities connected to violent extremism

- Harassment, profanity, and obscene language are all examples of inappropriate language.
- Promoting pharmaceuticals and other regulated substances, including their sale, use, and abuse
- Controversial or delicate topics and occurrences, such as those connected to war, political upheaval, catastrophes, and tragedies, even if graphic imagery is not displayed

However, the truth is that since 2012, YouTube has been automatically demonetizing content that it doesn't consider to be advertiser-friendly without giving the content creators any notice and without their consent.

The current state of affairs is preferable because creators are informed when their content is flagged and have the right to appeal any instance in which they believe a video was wrongfully banned from YouTube's advertising network.

Although advertising may be a popular way for creators to make passive income, the trade-off is that Google, the parent firm of YouTube, keeps about 45 percent of ad revenue.

To support their creative passion, YouTubers should look into alternative cash sources.

What Kinds of Videos Are Most Profitable?

I find humor, laughter, and such very enjoyable, given my personality. Compared to most other sorts of videos, comedic videos tend to go viral faster. So it seems that I would publish as many amusing videos as possible.

The next topic I want to explore is what you should do with your videos after implementing the monetization function. Tragic or dramatic types of videos will, of course, come in second to funny ones. You can tell this is accurate by regularly watching the evening news.

HOW TO INCREASE VIEWERS AND EARN MORE MONEY

There are a ton of techniques to increase the number of people who watch your YouTube videos, and I'll discuss a few of them here today, but I won't go into great detail because there are simply too many. Posting your videos on Facebook is the first step in getting many users to start watching them.

Your objective while using the internet is to go where the eyeballs are. Google, Facebook, and YouTube are currently the three most visited websites on the entire internet. Therefore, it is obvious that those three areas are where you want to direct traffic.

You may promote your new videos on Facebook to attract viewers. Here are just a few techniques you might employ:

- Post on your Facebook wall
- In groups on Facebook
- fan pages on Facebook
- SMS Text Messages
- Pay-per-click on Facebook
- posting a tagged photo or video

When you post a new video on your Facebook wall or in a Facebook group, those few ways will generate hundreds of visits. Of course, having many followers or friends on your page also influences the outcomes you get from using social media. The " Big Five" should be utilized in social media. The major five websites include places like:

- Facebook
- Twitter
- Pinterest
- Instagram
- Google+

The top five social media platforms above drive traffic to your most recent videos. Of course, the more viewers your videos receive, the more viewers will click on the ads that appear within them, ultimately resulting in more money in your bank account.

You will see some cash from the YouTube monetization scheme if you take the actions outlined in this chapter and start making tons of videos. Because your videos can be about anything, be careful not to make them too difficult for yourself.

One more piece of advice: You naturally excel at whatever you are most interested in. So simply take out your camera phone, choose a topic you enjoy discussing, and record yourself on your phone. It might truly be that easy.

Now that you know how to monetize your YouTube channel get out there and start creating plenty of videos! You will earn more the more you put in. Therefore, the task you can complete will be the one that comes to you the simplest.

How Many Youtube Views Are Required To Generate Income?

According to data from Influencer Marketing Hub, the typical YouTube channel may earn about $18 for every 1,000 ad views, which equates to between $3 to $5 for each video view.

The quantity of views you receive does not directly translate into money made. This is due to YouTube's requirements for paying advertisers: to get paid; a viewer must click an ad or watch the entire video ad (10, 15, or 30 seconds). You won't get paid if your video receives millions of views but no one sees it or clicks the advertisement.

You need four thousand view hours and one thousand subscribers to make money from your YouTube channel. When you're ready to start making money from your channel, you can join YouTube's Partner Program.

Affiliate marketing is one industry where you may start as a newbie and make money with few subscribers. Instead of getting paid for an ad click or a video watch, you can get paid when viewers buy affiliate products through your video. Popular topics for YouTubers include niches like cuisine reviews, product openings, and top [X] lists.

How Much Do Youtubers Earn Annually?

YouTubers generate more than $28.5 million in revenue annually from their channels. Smaller accounts can still support themselves on YouTube, even when they make large amounts of money.

Consider the YouTube channel for Justine Leconte. She helps people dress better and understand fashion on her channel, which has 913,000 subscribers and 91 million video views. Using only ad income, Influencer Marketing

Hub's YouTube Money Calculator estimates her total earnings to be around $259,304, or $979 per video.

According to these predicted figures, Justine might make a fortune by uploading one or two weekly videos to her YouTube channel. It's vital to remember that these are merely projections. Depending on the YouTube monetization techniques Justine employs for her business, she can make more or less than the abovementioned sums.

How Are Youtubers Compensated?

According to data from Forbes, advertisements account for 50% of the top YouTube earners' yearly income. Once you've established a YouTube channel, you may activate monetization and set up an AdSense account. Once your AdSense account balance reaches $100, you will only get paid.

Even if a YouTube channel doesn't have millions of subscribers, it can still be made money. Your earning potential is influenced by various factors, including the level of engagement you create, the niche you target, and the revenue streams you consider, in addition to the number of viewers and subscribers you have.

Second, you would believe that YouTube is the sole source of income based on this list of the top 10 earners. In actuality, each of these outlets carries a distinct product line. Before introducing their products, these channels first discovered and developed their consumers. Everyone should start by clearly defining their target demographic if making money on YouTube is part of their marketing strategy.

YOUTUBE SELLING ADVICE

Many monetization techniques include advertising campaigns or merchandise (e.g., crowdfunding a video series). But you'll want to watch out that your advertising doesn't undermine the integrity of your excellent content.

Many artists are quite concerned about "selling out." You can choose from various "placements" to advertise your items or campaigns. But you'll never get it if you never ask.

Recognize your YouTube audience

You are in a terrific position to monetize content in various ways when you build your audience. However, you won't be able to make the most of your opportunities until you are aware of who your audience is.

For many YouTubers trying to make money, having a more specialized channel will put you in a better position to collaborate with businesses that want to reach particular audiences (more on that later).

Be mindful of the following:

- The gender of your audience to determine if it leans more heavily toward any one group
- The age spectrum the majority of your viewers fall into
- The locations—countries or cities—where people are watching your videos
- overall viewership involvement, or "watch time."

You'll have a better grasp of your audience and be able to collaborate with companies if you have access to this demographic data. Your YouTube analytics can provide all demographic information, but try using a service like Social Blade to compare your channel to others.

Put a call to action on camera for your videos.

"If you liked this video, please click "Like" and "Subscribe."

Many YouTubers include a similar call to action after their videos to increase their viewing. Your audience is likelier to perform the desired action if you recommend it.

This strategy can be modified to focus your audience's attention on a chance to generate income.

Your videos should have well-timed YouTube cards.

YouTube Cards offer a striking approach to grabbing the attention of interested viewers, whether it's as part of an agreement with a company or you're promoting your items.

To maximize their impact, you can program them to appear at precisely the correct time, when they're most pertinent and least annoying.

In your video descriptions, provide links.

By including links to your video descriptions, you can direct viewers to your store, Patreon page, Kickstarter campaign, or other revenue-focused areas of your online presence.

Look at Unbox Therapy if you're a video artist who wants to concentrate on earning money as an affiliate marketer. Unbox Therapy focuses on product reviews and makes money from YouTube viewers by including affiliate links in the descriptions of its videos.

You can use "buy X get Y" promotions or discounts to entice new customers to purchase your products if you're making films promoting your products and you own or run a Shopify store.

Put your offer out there on different platforms.

Even though YouTube is where your content is hosted, you should still use all the other available distribution channels.

Share information about new campaigns or promotions on your Facebook, Twitter, and other social media accounts.

The more locations your message is present, the more likely it is to be seen. Therefore, using social media marketing to expand your audience outside YouTube is always a good idea.

The emergence of "YouTubepreneurs."

Rarely is money what drives the majority of creators to produce. The idea of creating something the entire world can appreciate. Many well-known YouTubers had modest beginnings, including PewDiePie, who produced videos as video game commentary.

Ironically, that puts them in a fantastic position to make money in a world where content is king.

Getting and holding their audience's attention is a challenge for many businesses, but YouTubers have already mastered it.

All that's left to do is use your imagination and entrepreneurial spirit to investigate ideas on how to make money off of your passion and audience.

HOW VIDEOS CAN HELP YOUR BUSINESS GROW

Videos are now essential for all sorts of businesses. A quality corporate video produced by one of the many companies that are now available will generate more new business than it costs. Even the tiniest businesses are utilizing videos to connect with current consumers and potential target customers, both online and in-store, as the cost of video production falls and the popularity of this type of advertising rises. Let's look at a few strategies for using videos to expand your business.

Promotional Videos

According to a 2011 Nielsen survey, videos are fifty times more likely than other types of material to appear on the first page of search engine results. Instead of reading through pages of text on a website or in a brochure to learn about a company's goods and services, many prospective buyers prefer to watch a brief video. A video is a useful tool for introducing yourself and your team and letting customers and clients get to know the people behind the company.

Instead of asking a consumer to sift through multiple photographs, you can demonstrate a variety of your work in a concise, amusing way that is more viewer-friendly. Always remember that online videos should not last longer than two or three minutes. Most viewers won't continue to watch for very long. Several quick, interesting videos are preferable to one long one. Inspire people to want more, not less.

Instructional Video

A person is more likely to buy, keep, and suggest a product to others if they are sure that they can easily assemble and utilize it. Online videos are a good technique to show customers how to use your products. Many people find it easier to follow visual instructions than step-by-step written instructions since they are less intimidating. You can show the various methods to use your product and make the most of it even if you don't sell something that needs instructions. Effective video editing is essential for the piece to remain at its ideal length and be simple to follow. You may create a how-to video that encourages customers to buy and utilize a product with the aid of a video production firm with experience in this area.

Lobby/In-Store Videos

Even if they are currently in your establishment, never pass up the chance to promote them to current clients. Give them something to look at other than their iPhone while they wait. More companies are coming up with ways to inform and entertain customers as people's attention spans get shorter and shorter, whether they are in a grocery store checkout line or pumping gas at a gas station. An in-store advertisement can be used to advertise discounts and new products that your consumers might not be aware of or to inform them of anything your company is doing to support the neighborhood.

Videos of client testimonials

What better medium exists than video to showcase client endorsements of your company? The impact is stronger when a prospective consumer witnesses someone praising your company than when they read a written testimonial. They are a close second to getting a personal endorsement from a friend or member of your family. A few brief client testimonies from various demographics that span a range of goods and services and how they satisfy the customers' needs can be a powerful marketing tool.

Increased Video Viewership

Keywords: If your video is online, it's important to draw viewers in with an attention-grabbing title that describes your company's actions. Keywords are essential for people looking for a service or product on the Internet to locate your company. Put keywords in the description and title fields. Make sure to link your website right at the top of the description.

SEO: Search engine optimization (SEO) is a separate economy sector. Professionals who know all the SEO gimmicks to get videos in front of the correct viewers work for several corporate video production companies.

Social media: In addition to your website, post your videos to all your social media channels, including Facebook, Twitter, LinkedIn, and Google+. Use a tool like TubeMogul to distribute them among other video hosting services. Put a link to your YouTube channel on your website, business cards, and printed marketing materials if you have one.

Remember to also send them to the folks on your email contact list.

Branding: Every video is a chance to spread the word about your company. In each one, your firm name and logo should be easily readable.

The use of video is increasingly essential for growing a business. Don't let the concept scare you. Nobody is anticipating a Spielberg video. They should look professional to inspire potential clients' confidence in you and your company. A skilled video production firm can ensure that your company is presented in the best possible way and reaches the greatest number of potential customers.

HOW TO MARKET YOUR CHANNEL

Video marketing often leads to quicker purchase decisions. A University of Pennsylvania study found that using video as a promotional tool increases customers' likelihood of purchasing by 72%. Compared to traditional marketing methods, prospects who watch the video have a better grasp of the service or product being promoted, which increases their likelihood of making a purchase and, as a result, increases the marketing budget's return on investment. According to industry studies, video promotions have response rates that are six times higher than, say, printed direct mail pieces.

Additionally, it moves quickly. The same study also reveals that 89 percent of customers will watch a video the day they receive it. If they like it, roughly 94 percent of those people will share it with a friend, coworker, or relative, which increases the likelihood that your message will spread like wildfire. Your video can take up the pace and carry your content once it's out there and shared in the appropriate internet communities and locations. This can only be terrific news if you have a fantastic video you're proud of.

How to Link to Your YouTube Channel Correctly for the Most SEO Link Equity

YouTube videos are frequently found on a variety of other websites. As online videos gain popularity, one of the video marketing methods is to promote YouTube channels by connecting to them on other websites to maximize link equity as more people view the channel. It's not as easy as just publishing the URL of your YouTube channel on different websites, though. You must spell out your YouTube channel's URL correctly.

So, what should the ideal YouTube channel URL look like to increase link equity? Instead of just youtube.com/TumbleweedTeam and its variants, the channel URL for Tumbleweed Team should be youtube.com/user/TumbleweedTeam. Do you notice the four-letter distinction? Despite directing people to your channel, the latter URL does not improve its page rank or link equity.

You'll see this URL in the address bar if you open your channel directly from YouTube rather than through an external link: youtube.com/user/TumbleweedTeam. So, that is the one that YouTube or Google can recognize.

Expert Justification

A website's most important section must be linked to the finest SEO techniques. It's crucial to do this so that all incoming links point to a single URL and boost the ranking of that website. The two Tumbleweed URLs were also mentioned to access the Tumbleweed YouTube channel. Therefore, the URL without "user" subtracts from the actual YouTube channel links. If all incoming links were attributed to the link using the proper URL structure (with "user"), the ranking would have been higher.

YouTube does not change the URL from 1) /Tumbleweed to 2) /user/Tumbleweed. And as was previously said, version #2 is the channel's default URL on YouTube. Therefore, the links to URL version #1 do not improve the YouTube channel's ability to rank. Web admins of other websites use canonical URLs to reroute alternative URL versions.

It is, therefore, preferable to utilize the URL that YouTube connects to ensure that all inbound connections increase the link equity of your YouTube channel. Be mindful of the format when you provide links to other websites online: YouTube.com/user/your channelaccountname.

Does It Work?

According to reports, videos with modified linking formats surged up to 25 rankings. Without a doubt, the growth is pretty big. Why not give it a shot? More online video marketing triumphs might be possible with other video marketing strategies.

How to Feature Your YouTube Video on YouTube's Front Page

You must, first and foremost, have a high-quality video if you want to maximize the traffic that comes to your YouTube channel. Find out what the audience wants by doing some study. Before you post the videos, involve your friends (but just those who can offer constructive comments). Encourage them to provide reviews as well. Because of this, your ranks will go up.

Keep in mind that the internet is expanding rapidly, and if you want to succeed, you must stay up to date with everything happening. To attract more traffic, you must be able to sell more and offer more high-quality videos.

Never be reluctant to ask viewers for their opinions. Let them know that you value their opinions and develop some original questions for them to respond to. The key is to get them there and keep them there. Make a strong enough impression for them to share your website with others. Create a distinctive presentation that will leave an impact. The secret is to think creatively.

Once you've made this impression, you must continue doing the same thing—if not better. Make sure to improve your YouTube channel to stand out. They'll constantly check in on you, and if you don't have anything brand-new, exciting, or distinctive to give, you'll soon fade into obscurity. Regularly adding videos to your website and improving your tags can help you stay on course. It doesn't hurt to do extra study and locate more techniques that can help you attract more viewers.

Make Your YouTube Videos More Popular!

You may already know how difficult it is to obtain views if you have videos on YouTube. Many people may upload videos hoping that hundreds of hits will flow automatically. They will be fortunate to receive a dozen views, and as the weeks go by, at most, a few more hits will start to dribble in. Rarely is this the case.

There are strategies to increase YouTube video views. Check out this advice:

1. **Friend and subscribe to as many individuals as you can.**

An excellent strategy for the network is to look for friends and join as many channels as possible before you publish any videos. You want to friend and subscribe to people whose style you genuinely appreciate or with whom you might have interests. When you subscribe to someone, they frequently do the same to check out what you have to offer. If you share similar likes, there is a good probability that they will watch your videos and perhaps share them with their friends, starting the snowball effect.

2. **Create a brief, humorous video.**

The most well-liked videos are humorous and brief. Most people visit these. Now, this need only serves as the inspiration for one of your videos. You can obtain more subscribers, friends, and views on future videos if you can entice viewers with a brief and humorous clip. Consider it an investment. One quick and lighthearted video will pay off by drawing more attention to and viewers to your other videos.

3. Employ A Service To Acquire Views.

Some websites provide services for obtaining views. To help you get over the initial hump of having a few people watch your videos, they will find friends and subscribers who share your interests or find other ways to boost your view counts. Once your views reach the tens of thousands, your content is rated higher, more people start to see it, and a snowball effect starts to happen where it keeps rising. However, you must first enter the region of a thousand views. Here, a service can be of great assistance.

SCALE YOUR VISION AND THINK DIFFERENTLY

How frequently do you visit YouTube each week? Or view a YouTube video that has been shared on Facebook? You probably watch them multiple times weekly if you're like most people. As one of the simplest ways to get traffic and attention to your website, YouTube is now used by millions of businesses for marketing. However, for YouTube marketing to be successful, some planning and willpower are needed. You have to scale your vision and think differently.

As a business owner, you must understand this is not a passing trend. Hundreds of organizations have attempted to use a video marketing approach but have encountered failure. What distinguishes one company's success with video marketing from another?

Some of the true success formulas that will assist you in developing a more effective YouTube strategy include the following:

Work hard and shrewd

If you've ever heard someone claim that video marketing was simple, they either misspoke or weren't being truthful and forthright. It is incredibly simple to be sucked into making new videos, and if you're not careful, you might squander valuable time making ineffective videos. You'll need to put your all into this method if you want to see a spike in website traffic, and you'll need to practice time management.

Pay Attention and React Suitably

The most successful YouTube marketers have discovered that the key to success is paying attention to your target audience's wants. What opinions are being expressed about your company? What comments have you received regarding your debut YouTube video? The following step is to respond to the input correctly. You must participate in the conversation about your company, whether the criticism is positive or negative. You are demonstrating your credibility to the customer by doing this. However, you must always respond responsibly and constructively. Anything less than this and disregarding criticism will only harm your business and you personally.

Do Something Different

Many companies just starting with YouTube marketing spend too much time trying to imitate what other companies are doing. Your company is in danger as a result of this. You need to try something wholly different instead. The videos that tend to become viral are unique ones. Consider things from a different perspective rather than browsing through YouTube videos to see what is possible for you to perform. Try watching other YouTube videos to see what hasn't been done before. This will boost your ranking and increase visitors to your website.

Develop Your Social Skills

Top YouTube marketers are active on social media and don't just read what others say. Set aside time each day to respond to other people's posts. How many posts on your Facebook page or Twitter account go unanswered? You must be social if you want to be effective in this marketing effort and win over the trust of your target audience. It only takes an hour a day to build this kind of credibility on the internet and show potential customers that you deserve their business.

Utilize video to increase anticipation

The finest video marketing strategies leverage suspense to keep viewers interested in their product or service. This requires some creativity, but it succeeds. It resembles any other regular television drama. Everyone is talking about it and wanting to discover what happens next because you left things on a cliffhanger. The key is to get their attention and make them want to know more.

Make it funny, and others will share your video.

People enjoy laughing, and anyone who claims differently is a secret humorist. People watch videos that make them laugh the most on social media. You should ensure that the humor you utilize in your video is honest. Anything deemed to be rude or excessively dry won't work. Whatever industry you are in, you should be able to find an amusing way to draw attention to your company.

Make use of SEO in your title and description.

Use keywords that will make your videos easier for your target audience to find when titling and describing them for your videos. It is similar to other marketing tactics in this regard. You should not fill your videos with too many keywords, though. You won't need to use all of them; just one or two will be enough to yield fruitful outcomes.

Popular YouTube videos often have sincere and amusing content that appeals to viewers. It is not feasible to become renowned by watching how-to videos. You could improve the ranking of your videos by brainstorming, writing down your ideas, and considering some techniques.

Although it is dead, YouTube Analytics is buried in your account. It is a summary of your channel that could be useful in determining the actions that your audience would like you to take. To encourage your audience to act, you should give them relevant and specific material that is of high quality and engages them in video and content marketing.

YOUTUBE MARKETING SECRETS.

These days, video-sharing services are extremely popular. YouTube operates! Everyone seems to have a YouTube marketing tip or resource to impart to other web viewers. And everyone enjoys making the most of our site for personal and professional reasons.

How can you make your product or video a huge hit on YouTube or other video-sharing websites if you have something you want to share? Some savvy video sharers have discovered some YouTube marketing secrets.

It's crucial to create or maintain fresh videos. You just don't upload your videos to the site and move on. You can take down the current video and submit it once more after some time to keep it fresh. This will give the impression that your video is original even when it has been "recycled." By including it in the "new videos list," you can draw viewers' attention to your video and perhaps drive traffic to your website.

Make sure you have a solid profile of friends, channel views, and subscribers before uploading videos to YouTube. These subscriptions, channel views, and friends would increase your online authority. Accounts with no connections may create or draw suspicion rather than clients.

Another YouTube marketing secret is understanding the influence of reviews, ratings, and views. Viewers- even customers- will watch again if you respond to comments or questions about the video. Other than the viewers themselves, no one else has the power to endorse and promote your videos. Being out of step with your target audience is not something you desire.

Social media websites can also be used to their full potential. Don't just leave your video on the website after you've uploaded it there. Without your promotion, it won't become well-known on its own. Another YouTube marketing trick is this. The emails of friends listed on your YouTube account can be used.

You can use the link to your YouTube-uploaded video in private messages to your friends on social media platforms. You can utilize their notice boards. Announcements about your video and the link can be posted. All of your friends on that particular social networking platform will see this. Therefore, if you belong to a site with 100 friends or contacts, that would be a significant promotional move.

Other YouTube marketing strategies include publishing your video in various formats and using names and tags similar to well-known videos. You can benefit from each video service's many formats and sizes. Your files can be saved as .flv, .avi, or .mov files.

You can save your video in two separate sizes in each format if you believe it to be important. As a result, your video would be distinctive in six different ways. No matter which of the various YouTube marketing strategies you choose to employ, make sure you create videos, or you won't be able to take advantage of this enormous free marketing resource.

Three Deadly YouTube Secrets You Must Know!

Getting some flyers and a set of business cards produced is no longer sufficient if you are running a business or considering doing so. YouTube is one of the many internet platforms that enables you to communicate and develop relationships with your audience around the clock. However, it is not as easy as just posting a video, so allow me to share:

Three YouTube secrets that are a must-know if you want to be seen

1. Target the Right Audience on YouTube

If you've ever posted a video for commercial purposes without a clear idea of your target audience, stop what you're doing now and refrain from creating any more videos until you do.

Users can find videos by entering a word or phrase into the search field. The YouTube search engine then looks for videos with the same description and displays them as results to the user. Even while this isn't the only aspect search engines take into account, the truth remains that if they don't know what the video is about, they won't even be able to include you in the search results.

You must utilize the keywords your audience will use to get included in this search. Put yourself in your audience's position and consider what your target consumer or potential user of your products or services would like to know. Consider any issues they might experience, any inquiries they might have, etc. Once you know your ideal customer, you can start to answer any questions they might have. The solutions you come up with will energize your video content and show you how to draw in the clients you desire most.

2. Send the appropriate message

The commercial pitch is not what YouTube is about. That is to say, it's not like a TV infomercial where you go straight to the salesperson. The YouTube viewer has a unique mentality. YouTube users need to be informed, entertained, and educated. Although it would be ideal to accomplish all three in a single video, your main focus should be on leaving the viewer with a lasting impression. You desire for them to leave, saying, "Wow! "That is a pretty wonderful idea! I never truly knew that! I want to learn more!"

Your main goal should be to use video to establish a connection with each customer and keep them coming back to your channel.

You stand a much better chance of the customer taking the following step if your messaging can address that fundamental requirement of the customer.

3. Direct your viewers to the next action

It's wonderful to have millions of viewers. It can give you a strong brand presence and a little rock star vibe. Rock artists, however, are only famous because they have sold out world tours and millions of albums. They wouldn't be able to live those ideal lifestyles or develop more music and gain more acclaim if they didn't generate revenue.

In keeping with the rock star analogy, videos should be made to satisfy viewers' appetites, leave them wanting more, and then persuade them to buy an album after they've downloaded a single and attend one of your global tour stops. How do you go about that? You should clearly state the next step you want the audience to take in each video's call to action at the end. Tell them if it's to see the next video in a series.

Your goals should center on gathering user data such as names and email addresses so that you can market to them using channels outside of YouTube that feature content they are interested in. You'll require the email for two main reasons.

- If your YouTube account is closed for any reason, you won't lose the connections you spent time cultivating.
- You now have two means to stay in touch with that individual (YouTube & email) as a result of receiving the email, allowing you to develop your relationship.

You now know my three YouTube secrets necessary to increase your audience, forge stronger bonds with your viewers, and increase your sales. Try them right now!

YOUR KEY MARKETING MESSAGE IS YOUTUBE ANALYTICS.

You may wonder who is watching your videos, where they are from, and to what age group they belong. Fortunately, YouTube Analytics can help. The capabilities on the YouTube platform are incredibly powerful.

Knowing who your audience is will enable you to produce content and marketing messages that are relevant to them. Prepared to meet them? When you select "demographics," the report will give you information about your audience's region and age range. Knowing your audience beforehand will enable you to think widely about the type of material you should produce and alter to engage with and address your target.

YouTube Analytics to improve your search engine ranking.

Are you happy with the viewership of your videos? If you check your Retention Rate, you might be startled to see how many visitors click away before your video is finished. You could believe that your audience loves and appreciates your material. You may find out the typical duration of each video using the Retention Rate. This section of your Analytics is crucial—in fact, all of them!—because that is what Google utilizes to determine whether your video is fascinating or uninteresting.

Higher search rankings for higher retention rates! Remember that. Shorter videos can enhance the likelihood that viewers will stick around for the whole thing. If a video is too long, consider your behavior as a viewer. You might decide to skip a scene or end the video altogether. Right? You must consider your audience's interests, and once you know what information they are seeking, you should be able to produce material that meets their needs.

Using YouTube Analytics to increase website traffic is Possible!

When running a business, finding methods to increase traffic and create leads from your website is important. The solutions are already available if you run a YouTube channel and need to generate leads. You could absolutely and confidently drive traffic from your videos to your website using YouTube Analytics. How? One of the incredible secrets of your YouTube channel is this section.

Have you ever seen a YouTube video with pop-up ads? They're annotations, right? It looks like a call-to-action box on top of the video, which could anger viewers because it might obscure their view. However, YouTube Annotations can convert your viewers into leads and sales if you use them properly.

You can identify the period when engagement is high and the point where most viewers click away from your video using YouTube Analytics, which gives you the pitons and dunk for your content. This is the plan: Find the point where your viewers finish watching your content and place the annotation with a link to your website there. Make sure to place it 10 seconds before they leave, just before the drop, including an "Associated Website" annotation with a clear call to action to encourage readers to click it. Start generating leads from numerous of these "exit peoples"! Watch as the addition of annotations to your videos effectively increases traffic to your websites and generates leads.

Increasing the conversion of your annotations? The answer is YouTube Analytics!

YouTube Analytics' most useful tool, "Click Through Rates," includes your annotations. It is possible to see which annotations relate to your material and which do not as soon as you are located inside Annotation Analytics. The ability to monitor click-through rates for each annotation is now available to you. You can: By utilizing this functionality, you can:

You can perceive and quantify the success of conversion, as well as the failure of conversion, by adjusting the duration of annotations.

Copy your annotations and change or alter them to reflect the difference you observe.

Utilize YouTube Analytics to gather information for your paid advertisements.

Regarding paid advertising, use YouTube Analytics to design, alter, and produce the marketing message to specify your targeting. Determining which videos have had the most views and are the most popular. Additionally, you'll discover which and what kinds of content your viewers enjoy. From there, you can develop advertisements that will be a hit and ignite interest in your market, whether with

YouTube, Facebook, or Twitter, all of which offer highly effective ways to promote your brand and company. This strategy will also help you improve the return on your advertising investments.

As you are aware, YouTube Analytics gives you the following details about your audiences:

- Location
- Age Groups
- Gender

All the data you can find in your analytics is helpful for the YouTube videos and other material you plan to produce. Additionally, it will give you more advanced-level insights into your YouTube content, marketing initiatives, or other social media platforms, which should help you improve traffic, generate leads, and eventually boost revenue for you and your company.

Are You Unknowingly Sending Your YouTube Viewers to Your Competitors? - YouTube Profit Secret

The results are: YouTube is a strong ally in expanding your brick-and-mortar or online business. Skeptical? Then consider these astounding details:

The second-ranked web search engine right now is YouTube. YouTube is the most popular video-sharing website. Therefore if you don't have videos, you are missing out on millions of searches made by your ideal customers and clients. The competition is not even close.

YouTube is no longer simply for people who have too much free time. Both small business owners and multinational corporations use it as a serious business tool.

If you don't watch out, YouTube can give your rivals a large portion of your audience.

Why is this:

When you use YouTube's simple copy-and-paste embed option to add a video to your website, clickable thumbnails for many additional videos are displayed once your video has finished playing. Consequently, viewers who click on them can leave your blog, website, or another place where the video was embedded. However, there is an easy way to prevent this oversight and keep all of your views to yourself.

Visit the page where the YouTube video you just submitted is first.

Second, there is a gray box with a text field labeled Embed near the top of the page to the right of your video. You can copy and paste this to have your video appear on your blog or website.

But hold on! You now take a further step to ensure you aren't sending your audience to your rivals. There is a little button with what appears to be blue gear to the right of the Embed text box. When you click it, several choices will be presented. One of them is the Include-related videos checkbox.

Keeping visitors on your website and boosting the likelihood that they will buy from you. Ensure that this box is not ticked. This is important: A checkmark in the Included related videos box must be removed. This automatically modifies the embed code so viewers can only choose to replay your video after it has finished playing.

The truth is that your clients aren't just responding to your online video marketing; they anticipate it. And by being aware of a few basic tricks like this, you can ensure that your videos pay back many times the time you invested in making them.

Although you might not be aware of it, there are countless minor adjustments and straightforward keys like this that you can employ to propel your organization with online video.

YOUTUBE SECRETS: HOW TO USE YOUTUBE MARKETING TO START A TIDAL WAVE OF SALES

Have you got anything to sell, either a product or a service? With YouTube marketing, you can significantly boost your monthly revenues if you have a well-known website and are trying to offer a certain good or service. This type of marketing has the benefit of putting you in direct contact with potential clients, allowing them to view your items in action before making a purchase.

Demonstrations in video Boost Products Sales

People are more inclined to purchase when they can experience a product's benefits than when they can only read about them. If a visitor sees a photo and a brief description of your products on your website, they might want to buy them but still be on the fence. However, they would be more likely to buy the product from you if they could watch a full video demonstration.

You may create quick video demos of your goods using YouTube marketing. You could even utilize the product to demonstrate how it functions and is used in the video. Then, to boost your sales, you may post these videos along with the descriptions of your products on your website. You can accomplish this quickly and easily, and it will help you connect with more people worldwide.

YouTube marketing, previously only utilized for fun, is now a crucial component of any effective marketing plan. Millions will see this video of individuals who enjoy browsing YouTube in addition to visitors to your website. This implies that viewers of your YouTube videos could potentially visit your website and learn about additional goods and services they might consider acquiring, even if it's later.

Learn How To Increase Website Traffic With YouTube Videos

YouTube draws hundreds of millions of visitors each month who use the platform to look for information about businesses and a wide range of topics. You should consider the advantages of using YouTube to market your business if you want to increase website traffic and monthly income.

You should think about producing and publishing promotional videos on YouTube if your objective is to increase traffic to your website or blog to expand your business. When they upload videos to YouTube, professionals, individuals, and business owners can profit from limitless traffic without spending any money.

Streaming Performance

To see at least snapshots of your channel performance, click "overview" Because you wanted to make sure that you would have as much engagement from YouTube as your anticipated goal, this section might require the most thought. Some of the key resources on your initial path to success include traffic, subscribers, and content monetization.

Before beginning, familiarize yourself with all there is to know about YouTube.

Given the high advertising costs, many online marketers are devoting time to learning about effective YouTube marketing tactics and video marketing strategies that companies worldwide employ. Enrolling in YouTube marketing training is one of the greatest ways to learn everything there is to know. Although numerous books are produced on the subject, the fastest way to learn everything you need to know about utilizing YouTube to sell your business is to enroll in a video course on how to effectively and efficiently market on YouTube.

Videos Can Teach Successful Internet Marketers and Business Owners New Tricks

Books are not nearly as useful as training videos. You should consider watching a YouTube training video if you're just starting with YouTube or if you've been using it for a while but aren't getting the desired results. Another option you can consider is enrolling in a YouTube crash course, training on YouTube, or watching one or more YouTube videos. You will then be well on your approach to discovering all the YouTube tricks you require to utilize the website efficiently.

Those who invest the time to learn from the experts will discover all there is to know about YouTube promotion and other video marketing techniques, including but not limited to increasing your YouTube views and directing more YouTube traffic to your websites and blogs.

Due to its widespread popularity, YouTube is one of the greatest places to conduct marketing.

NEW YOUTUBE FEATURES

Since Chad Hurley, Steve Chen, and Jawed Karim launched YouTube in 2005; millions have watched, rewatched, and shared videos from around the world. Google owns YouTube after buying it in 2006.

The powerful content distribution platform helps content creators and advertisers connect and inspire others. YouTube is constantly updating and improving its software for the masses.

Since Google added YouTube videos to search results, more people have migrated to YouTube. Businesses and influencers are making fortunes by attracting YouTube audiences.

YouTube knows how to keep its audience engaged with updates for creators and viewers.

Here are recent YouTube updates and features.

HANDLES

YouTube introduced "handles" on October 10, 2022, which are creators' '@names' across platforms.

YouTube will display the unique account name on channel pages and Shorts. Users can tag the handle in comments, video descriptions, collaborations, and titles.

Channel names aren't handles. YouTube said handles would identify a channel another way.

Unlike channel names, handles are unique to each channel so that creators can establish their brand on YouTube.

YouTube said the feature would be rolled out soon, and creators will be notified when it's available for their channels; personalized URLs will have the same name by default, but creators can change it if they want.

UNSKIPPABLE ADVERTISEMENTS

YouTube is testing a new feature that shows five non-skippable ads before playing a video.

YouTube responded to a user's complaint about forced ads on September 8, 2022, via its official Team YouTube Twitter account.

"This may happen with 6-second bumper ads. You can send feedback via YouTube's send feedback tool, "YouTube said.

This may happen with 6-second bumper ads. You can send YouTube feedback using the send feedback tool.

Gizmochina reported on September 13 that users complained about unskippable ads.

The report says YouTube free users are testing unskippable ads, not YouTube Premium users. This has led to rumors that YouTube may increase subscriptions to YouTube Premium.

Not all YouTube free users see the five ads, indicating the system is still being tested.

ZOOM IN, ZOOM OUT

YouTube's Premium mobile app is testing pinch-to-zoom. 9to5Google reports that the opt-in feature works in portrait and landscape modes. The video can be zoomed in for clarity.

YouTube tested the feature until September 1, 2022, to gather user feedback and make changes. After YouTube makes any needed tweaks, the feature will roll out widely.

IMPROVING OVERSIGHT

Under supervised accounts, parents can restrict under-13 children's access to videos and music. They can choose features, account settings, and ads for their kids.

In January 2022, YouTube announced that supervised accounts can now use the video-sharing platform on eligible smart T.V.s and other devices as an app or through the web browser. Children with supervised accounts can also use the YouTube Music app.

Parents can use YouTube, YouTube Kids, and YouTube Music on Google Assistant-enabled devices in the U.S.

Introducing Shorts

Short videos are popular. Instagram Reels and Facebook Reels are popular because people prefer short videos. YouTube added 'Shorts' in 2020. YouTube Shorts has 5 trillion all-time views, per its blog.

In February 2022, all Android devices could create Shorts by importing 60-second horizontal video clips from their galleries.

In March, iPhone improved this feature so users can improve Short lighting. Tap 'More Minimize' in the iPhone camera toolbar to find the 'Lighting' icon. You can now edit videos in real-time. Tap the 'Retouch' magic wand in your phone's camera toolbar to smooth skin. Both features remain until manually disabled.

Watch Shorts on your computer, laptop, tablet, and phone. On a tablet or phone, tap the Shorts icon at the bottom of the YouTube app or browser.

YouTube Studio Editor

YouTube updated Studio Editor in February to support video creators. Users can easily add video thumbnails, end screens, audio tracks, and info cards.

Videos can be trimmed and blurred. This refinement simplifies YouTube video editing.

Subtitle Editors

YouTube's Subtitle Editor channel permission allows creators to delegate subtitle creation to others.

Subtitle Editors' access was improved in April. Creators can let trusted users add and edit subtitles on their videos and change default-language subtitles.

NEW RESEARCH TAB

Creators can use YouTube Analytics to gauge their channels' performance and create more appealing content.

YouTube's new 'Research' feature lets you see what viewers have searched for in the last 28 days. Similar channel searches, content gaps, and search volume can be filtered by geography and language.

Sign into your YouTube studio account and click 'Analytics' on the left menu. Select 'Research' and type a topic or term in the search bar. You can also view Google Trends, report, or unsave a search.

YouTube will add more languages soon.

'INCREASE STRICTNESS'

YouTube Studio now lets creators moderate inappropriate video comments.

In the optional 'Increase strictness' setting, you can review more comments, especially when creators find inappropriate content on their channels.

Changes

YouTube strengthened its harassment and cyberbullying policy in April. You can't share medical records and other personal information.

It also created a guideline called 'Inappropriate content for kids and families to tailor ads for children. It includes 'Content that encourages negative behavior,' 'Mature content aimed at kids,' and 'Shocking content aimed at kids.'

CONCLUSION

More marketers than ever are getting involved in video's transformation of the digital marketing landscape. Why? Customers want to see more of it, so that's a start. Additionally, 88 percent of video marketers claim that the medium has a positive return on investment. Because of this, 95% of marketers who use video plan to expand their investment in the upcoming months.

It's time to create a video presence for your business if it doesn't already have one. Making a YouTube channel is among the finest strategies to achieve that.

Made in United States
North Haven, CT
19 November 2022